...on course to the stars

1/28

...on course to the stars

THE ROGER B. CHAFFEE STORY

as told to

C. DONALD CHRYSLER

by

DON L. CHAFFEE AND FAMILY

KREGEL PUBLICATIONS, Grand Rapids, Michigan

Library of Congress Catalog No. 68-15565

*A portion of the royalties from the sale of
this book have been designated to be chan-
neled into the Central High School (Grand
Rapids) and Purdue University (Lafayette,
Indiana) Roger B. Chaffee Memorial
Scholarship Funds.*

First Edition

Printed in the United States of America

Author's Acknowledgments

The Author gratefully expresses thanks to:

Don L. Chaffee and family, who gave liberally of their time and effort to supply information necessary for the writing of this book.

Martha Chaffee, widow of Roger B. Chaffee, who related many of the experiences given in the book.

Bob Day, staff member, *Grand Rapids Press*, who assisted in many ways.

Thomas Lane and other personnel in the Public Affairs Office, John F. Kennedy Space Center, Florida who assisted materially in providing information used herein.

Gearldean Chrysler, who spent many hours in typing of initial draft of book.

Merle, my wife and manuscript editor, who also contributed many hours in research and typing of this manuscript, and without whose help this book would not have been possible.

Publisher's Acknowledgments

The Publisher wishes to express appreciation to the following:

1. *Editorials*

   WOOD Radio, AM/FM/TV, Grand Rapids, Michigan
   WRLD Radio, Lanett, Alabama
   for permission to use material quoted from editorials

2. *Excerpts*

   NASA (National Aeronautics and Space Administration), Manned Spacecraft Center, Houston, Texas, *Roundup* Magazine, for permission to use quotation from Paul Haney's write-up, July 8, 1964.

   Purdue University News Service, Lafayette, Indiana, for material quoted from the Flight Log of Roger B. Chaffee, appearing in the *Purdue University News*.

   United Press International, New York, for use of news dispatch from Houston, October 19, 1963

3. *Photographs*

   Associated Press, New York
   Grand Rapids Press, Grand Rapids, Michigan

   NASA, Manned Spacecraft Center, Public Affairs Office, Houston, Texas;

   Newspaper Enterprise Association, Cleveland, Ohio, cartoon, "Stairway to the Stars";

   Purdue University News Service, Lafayette, Indiana, photograph of Chaffee Flight Log;

   Wide World Photos, New York
   for permission to use the many pictures included in photo inserts.

4. *Poems*

   Donald L. Chaffee, Wyoming, Michigan:
   "Roger B. Chaffee"; "Your Passage Through This Life";

   Blanch Chalmers Niewiadomski, Grand Rapids, Michigan:
   "Mission Accomplished"; also the title, . . . ON COURSE TO THE STARS, was taken from her poem, "Achilles Heel," not in this book.

   S. Louise Rayle, Traverse City, Michigan: "A Salute to Our Astronauts."

5. *Prologue*

   Jennifer Mitchell Brown, Kokomo, Indiana, author of the Prologue, who has graciously given her permission for use of the material herein.

Foreword

I was pleased and honored when Roger Chaffee's father, Don, asked me to read this book in manuscript form and to comment on it in a foreword to the published work.

I was honored because Roger Chaffee is one of this Nation's great modern-day heroes, a man who gave his life for his country just as surely as have those Americans who have died on the battlefield.

It pleased me because there were similarities between Roger Chaffee's life and mine that always made me feel close to him. We both grew up in Grand Rapids, Michigan. We were members of the same Boy Scout troop, although in different time spans. We both became Eagle Scouts, played football in high school and served in the Navy as lieutenant commanders.

Roger Chaffee's story, as told in this book by his family and friends, is a warm and intimate account of a hero's life. It is a highly personalized story, rich in remembrance and anecdote. No reader can fail to be touched by it.

There is irony in this story, as when Roger said in an 11th grade theme regarding the choice of nuclear physics as a vocation: "There are practically no physical hazards, outside of the usual chance of burned hands and fingers, except maybe one chance in a thousand of radiation poisoning."

One of the most touching moments in this book comes in a

letter Roger Chaffee wrote in 1963 to the son of a man he worked under at a Grand Rapids department store. In telling this eight-year-old how he became an astronaut, Roger said, "You have to love your country so much that every time you see our flag you feel warm inside."

This book makes clear the tremendous personal drive that gave Roger Chaffee the thrust he needed to win astronaut ranking.

A high school senior class friend of his recalls that like an actor who strives to see his name in lights, Roger said he wanted his to be in the history books. He wanted to be the first man on the moon. This was four years before the Russians launched their first Sputnik.

But this book makes clear it was far more than personal ambition that made Roger Chaffee an astronautical pioneer who gave his life to the U.S. space program. Interviewed by newsmen after being named an astronaut, Roger said, "I'll be doing something for my country — something in which I can take pride."

Apart from giving the reader an intimate glimpse of Roger Chaffee, boy and man, this book offers a non-technical and personal account of astronaut survival tests and preparations for the abortive and tragic Apollo manned space effort in which Roger Chaffee died along with Astronauts Gus Grissom and Ed White.

We all know that Roger Chaffee was "shooting for the moon" and instead found a place in the stars.

To me the true significance of this book is that it tells a story of family life which carries a lesson for all America. It reflects the importance of the family as a foundation for a healthy America.

It might well be said that if all family households in our Nation were as happy and harmonious as was the Chaffees, many of America's problems simply would not exist.

This is more than the story of a man. It is the story of a hero and his family, and it is well worth reading.

Gerald R. Ford

The House of Representatives
Washington, D.C.

Contents

Foreword ix

Prologue xiii

1. The Quarantine Baby — And How He Grew . . . 15

2. Readin', Writin', 'n 'Rithmetic 23

3. The Good Scout 41

4. Joe College 53

5. Martha and the Flying Machines 61

6. Navy Man 71

7. "Dad, I'm In!" 79

8. . . . On Course 97

9. The Making of an Astronaut 105

10. Last Preparations 113

11. Count-down T Minus 10 121

12. "Three Valiant Young Men . . ." 127

13. In Memoriam 135

14. Aftermath 149

Cartoon 154

Glossary 155

Roger B. Chaffee

"From somewhere in the distance I hear the bugle's call,
'Tis the notes of the last farewell over the darkened pall.
He gave his life for peace, some soldier for his land,
And now to silent slumber, he's laid with reverent hand.

"The dying notes of the bugle ring out so fair and clear,
As if to whisper to him that he has naught to fear.
And while the sun is sinking and setting in the Golden West,
It casts a farewell shadow over the soldier's rest."

Written by Donald L. Chaffee, the father, following the spacecraft tragedy.

Prologue

January 27, 1967, Cape Kennedy, Florida . . . It was a seemingly typical Friday at Cape Kennedy. The mild winter winds blew softly and carried a whisper of the activity on Pad 34.

Cradled in its gantry was a powerful Saturn I-B rocket, unfueled, but waiting . . . waiting for the countdown of a simulated launch. In just eighteen days this mighty giant was expected to soar from its pad into the mysterious realms of outerspace; the first manned flight of the project known as Apollo. Eventual destination — the moon.

Perched atop the twenty-two story rocket was a comparatively small white capsule bearing a colorful painting of the American flag, the words "United States" stenciled clearly just above it.

Inside the capsule, preparing for the simulated liftoff were three men, the prime crew of Apollo 204, courageous and proud in their roles.

The test began at 1:00 p.m. EST with the entry of the silvery suited spacemen into the cabin. At 2:50 p.m., the hatch was closed and sealed, and the cabin filled with oxygen. The men relaxed in individual contour couches and they, too, waited.

The test had already been delayed due to a malfunction of the oxygen and communications systems, and outside the command module, 220 feet off the ground, technicians doggedly worked, monitoring test equipment and making last minute adjustments.

Adjacent to the launch pad, 1,000 feet away, was the blockhouse where other technicians and NASA officials were gathered to view the happenings over a closed circuit telemetry monitor.

"T minus 10," a voice boomed out from the concrete structure, indicating the wait was nearly over and the simulated takeoff close at hand.

Now, 6:31 p.m. EST — a brilliant white flash!

"Fire in the spacecraft!" cried a voice from within the capsule.

The television monitors and all communications went dead. Dense smoke poured from the hatch as workmen rushed up the 250-foot steel gantry in a high speed elevator in an attempt to save the astronauts. Twenty-seven men were overcome by the bitter black smoke and intense heat, and it took nearly five endless minutes to pry open the charred metal door of the cabin . . . Too late . . .

Americans were stunned by the loss of their heroes, Virgil Grissom, Edward White II, and Roger B. Chaffee. The nation, and indeed the world, mourned.

Since that tragedy on the launchpad, countless pages have been written eulogizing the three comrades and speculating as to the cause of the fire. A board comprised of highly qualified experts, after weeks of intensive investigation, revealed that a single electrical spark is thought to have touched off the burst of flame. The exact cause may never be known.

Roger, Gus Grissom, and Ed White knew and accepted the dangers of their chosen life. They were pioneers of space, and the universe was waiting to be conquered.

"If we die, we want people to accept it. We are in a risky business and we hope that if anything happens to us, it will not delay the program. The conquest of space is worth it."

These words were spoken by Lieut. Commander Grissom, but their meaning was shared by each of the astronauts.

The purpose of this book is not to ponder the whys and wherefores of the disaster. It is our desire to introduce you to Roger Chaffee, youngest of the three Apollo spacemen. This is his story, told by those who knew and loved him.

1

The Quarantine Baby — And How He Grew

One fine, spring day in 1944, several boys stood or knelt in varying positions over a concentrated game of marbles. Their concentration was not so great, however, that they missed the throbbing sound of a large plane passing overhead. It was war time, and such planes passed rather frequently. One of the boys jumped up, his eyes scanning the sky until he located the fast-disappearing plane. He spoke positively to the others, in a voice that had a ring of prophecy, "I'll be up there flying in one of those someday." And they believed him.

Roger Chaffee had left a card table covered with parts of model airplanes to join the other boys for a game of marbles. But airplanes were his first love. They had been for most of his nine years. The card table in the Chaffee living room had become a permanent fixture, while Roger and his father, Don L. Chaffee, worked on the various types of models. Don had been a barnstorming pilot in a Waco 10 biplane in 1930 and had passed his own love of planes along to his son. As barnstorming pilot of the ninety horse-powered, Curtis Wright-engined plane, Don had flown at fairgrounds and carried passengers for hire.

He also had piloted stunting parachute jumpers, rather a novelty in those days of the 1930's.

Don frequently took the family to visit the Grand Rapids airport, and there they would analyze the take-offs and landings of the many planes. On more than one occasion, Roger would comment, "*That* one set down pretty hard, didn't it Dad?"

Roger built his first model airplane in the fourth grade. Don set up the table in the living room, and Roger began cutting the curved wing ribs and other parts out of balsa wood. The ribs were then attached to balsa strips, and the wings and body took shape. The completed frame was covered with tissue paper and painted. A few decals added the finishing touch. It was a thing of beauty to Roger, although only the first of many others he built.

Roger's first interest in airplanes was born in his very first years. He was shown how to take a piece of paper and fold it several times to make a plane — nose, wings and tail. He would throw it exuberantly across the room and then watch with much glee while it circled and glided, especially when eventually its crashing brought it zooming down past someone's ear! Straight pins sometimes were stuck into the nose of a well-performing model, adding weight and additional "looping" to the little plane.

After this had come new, more complicated models, models constructed with balsa wood and covered with tissue paper shrunk onto the frame with banana oil. Rubber bands attached to the propellor served as the motor. This was before the time of ready-made kits, and Don whittled and shaped the propellors himself.

Around this time Don built Roger's first outdoor flying model, with a wingspread of over thirty inches. It was a perfect "flyer." Even after the prop stopped turning, it would glide a long way. One time it flew for half a block, and Roger was so excited that his mother had him pose for a picture, missing front teeth and all, holding the prize airplane.

But to get the complete story of Roger B. Chaffee, it is necessary to begin at the beginning . . .

Roger Chaffee's birth, as his death, was surrounded by circumstances one could hardly refer to as ordinary.

In that January of 1935, the Chaffee family consisted of Don, Blanche (affectionately called Mike), and Donna, aged two years and two months. Their home was located in Greenville, Michigan, thirty miles northeast of Grand Rapids. They were a *family* in the true sense of the word and, as such, were eagerly awaiting the addition of a new member.

That month before Roger's birth was one to be remembered by the Chaffee family. It began as a typical Michigan January; sometimes snowy, sometimes thawing, but windy, cold, and beautifully white!

Not many days of low temperatures are required to form strong layers of ice on Michigan's many lakes and streams. With the ice come the winter sportsmen, eager for ice fishing — a pleasant pastime if one has a willing spirit and a warm coat. The Chaffees had both. They had spent many hours together in such a pastime. But now Don would go alone, for Mike felt the time had come for her to withdraw from these activites and wait in a more sedate manner for the birth of their second child.

Any ice fisherman will tell how comforting a little fire in the shanty can be. And Don, being a knowledgeable sportsman, gathered twigs from along the shoreline for his shanty fire. Being somewhat less than knowledgeable about botany, he also gathered some poison sumac branches.

A few days later a red rash began to appear on his hands and feet. Poison sumac with a vengeance! But with the assistance of the family doctor and a prescription from the corner drug store, the rash disappeared in a week or so, and things in the Chaffee household returned to normal.

This lasted for only a few days, however. A short time later Don became ill again. Without deep concern, the poison sumac treatment was begun again, but his temperature soared and a rash appeared all over his body. The doctor's somber diagnosis was delivered in a tone that told the seriousness of the situation. Don had Scarlet Fever! Mike, expecting a child in a matter of weeks, was now exposed to a disease much dreaded in those years of the 1930's!

Community health rules would not allow her to keep her prearranged appointment at the Greenville hospital, and to deliver a baby into that quarantined household was unthinkable. Fast action between the doctor and the Department of Health brought permission for Mike and Donna to move to the home of Mike's parents in Grand Rapids. Within hours the move was accomplished, and in that time of confusion and worry, it was comforting for Mike to know that she was to be with her mother when the baby was born.

Roger Bruce Chaffee was born a long two weeks later in his maternal grandparents' home on the northeast side of Grand Rapids. Although not a large baby, he weighed in at a healthy 6 lbs., 8 oz., and was 19" long. The date was February 15, 1935. His mother's recorded comment: "Everything went well."

Ten days passed before Don, finally released from quarantine, was able to travel to Grand Rapids to see his new son. It was a proud father who finally returned to Greenville with his family, now including little three-week-old Roger.

According to the well-kept records in his baby book, Roger, a chubby, brown-eyed blond, developed normally and in due course began to show his own strong personality. The last entry by age was made at two years: "Very persistent, and doesn't easily forget little things."

Persistence was a characteristic noted early by his parents and evidenced throughout his lifetime. From stroller to spacecraft he displayed an unswerving determination to achieve his goals. His mother recalls his eager attention to her floor-scrubbing chore even before his second birthday. Because his fascination with the pail of scrub water prolonged her job, she thought she could bar him from the room by placing his highchair across the doorway. This she did, but discovering that shaking and hollering would not remove the obstacle, he reconnoitered the situation, then quietly made his way through the chair rungs. After this accomplishment, the floor-cleaning detail was done during Roger's nap time. His obsession with the living room floor lamp was equally trying, and the lamp shade was replaced more than once when the enterprising toddler evaded his mother's watchful eye.

The Chaffee family grew into a closely knit unit as family patterns were established during the children's early years. After each evening meal, the living room floor became a playland. Mom, Dad, Donna and Roger rolled balls, pushed cars, wrestled and together built castles of blocks to be tumbled down amid childish chuckles. Such play continued until the children outgrew this sort of fun-time and Mom and Dad could no longer stand the pace.

As Roger and Donna grew older, story time became a part of the pattern of their lives, nursery rhymes and stories becoming so familiar that the readers dared not short cut. These bedtime reading sessions were considered beneficial, especially when they followed the roughhousing, and they were continued through the years, the material changing as the children grew and their interests broadened. Grandfather Chaffee, retired, often found time to take them to the Greenville Library where they were introduced to a wider world of books. They loved these excursions and often renewed two or three times a book which they particularly enjoyed.

The reading hour was a profitable time, as Roger and Donna developed not only interest and knowledge, but also a very real sense of security. They were loved and this love was made evident. The children enjoyed true comradship with Mom and Dad Chaffee.

About the only spankings received by Roger were for running into the street. It did not take long for him to deduce that a warm stern meant no curb-stone sitting! Once, when Roger rose from a nap, in high spirits, he started off from the front porch for a trot down the sidewalk toward the curb. His parents watched to see how far he would go. Suddenly he cried out, turned and headed for the sanctuary of his mother's arms. But it wasn't a change of purpose; they discovered that a bee had stung the end of his nose! The Chaffees thought with secret amusement that he must have felt this a rather severe way of teaching him to stay out of the street.

A handful of dandelions was a common summertime gift for his mother. With a pleased look on his small face, Roger would press the oftimes wilted bouquets into Mike's hand with the words, "Look, Mom, flowers!" On one occasion, he appeared with a few flowers from the neighbor's garden. For these he was warmly thanked and then given a little lecture on respect for the property of others.

On his third birthday Roger received a cart and immediately manifested his persuasiveness by talking Donna into pulling him back and forth on the walk in front of the house. He also had a rocking horse and loved to deck himself out in his cowboy suit. With his hat, vest, chaps and guns, he would mount his horse and become, in his own eyes, a real cowboy like the Lone Ranger.

Sundays were enjoyable days for the Chaffee family as they found an unending variety of things to do. Often they would pick up the grandparents and go for a ride, on a picnic or take a longer ride out to the children's great grandmother's farm. Roger and Donna were allowed to feed the chickens there, each carrying a small dish of corn and scattering it on the ground. Roger, not much taller than the chickens, really did not appreciate this "privilege" and was sometimes a little slow in doling out the corn. The chickens would follow him in eager anticipation, squawking and clucking, as he slowly backed away. Finally, thoroughly intimidated by the advancing flock, he would throw the remainder of the corn at them, turn and run for the house as fast as his sturdy legs could carry him!

The children had their favorite roads and recreation sites, and one of their most loved spots was Wabasis Creek, in the northeastern section of Kent County. Here the waters were clear and cold, and the trees large and friendly. Limited fishing equipment was always carried in the Chaffee car, and occasionally the children would catch a small fish. Their shouts of glee brought smiles of amusement and pleasure to those within hearing distance, which at times seemed to include a mile!

At the age of four, Roger was baptized in the Greenville Methodist Church and was considered by his parents well mannered enough to have more outside-of-the-home contacts. He was then allowed to go to Sunday School, accompanied by Donna and his parents. Colorful pictures of Bible scenes, awarded for each Sunday's attendance, were carefully collected and prized by Roger and were a source of great delight to him.

The Tulip Festival at Holland, Michigan, was an annual family outing. The children enjoyed the beautiful gardens there and the displays of the miniature canals, boats, buildings and farms. The colorful acres of tulips and the sound of wooden shoes striking the pavement were sights and sounds happily remembered by all the Chaffees.

In 1940 their visit to the Holland tulip festival was not as gay as usual, for it reminded the older Chaffees that Hitler had invaded the original land of tulips and windmills, his armies overspreading that lovely country. Who could look at these beautiful tulips and rejoice when the flowers in the land of Holland bloomed amidst destruction and suffering. But the Chaffee children were too young to be aware of war. Theirs was still a world of peace and well-being, and the concern as to this country's possible involvement in the conflict was felt only by their parents.

Even by December 7, 1941, Roger, not quite six, and Donna, only eight, could not comprehend the grimness of the hour when news broadcasts on that dark Sunday told of the bombing of Pearl Harbor by Japanese planes. America was now forced into the conflict. The war brought many changes in the life of every American family. Gas-rationing went into effect, along with sugar-rationing. Lengthy family trips had to be curtailed because of the gas-rationing. Mike had to figure out ways to feed her family using less sugar and even less butter!

In Greenville the children none the less found many happy hours of recreation, recreation that was close to home. A huge house, which they called the "mansion," was under construction about a half block from the Chaffee home and was a place of consuming interest. It was a favorite pastime for Roger, Donna and their friends to spend hours on the site watching the builders. It was exciting to wander through the nearly completed home, marveling at the *seven* bathrooms (their house had one!) each in a different color. It seemed to them to be a fairy-land house. One day they were told by the workers that they could not return. Bitterly disappointed, the children looked elsewhere for adventure and discovered a "haunted" house across the street from the Chaffee home. With both dread and anticipation, the Chaffee children and their playmates would creep quietly up to peer through the grimy windows. It became a contest to see who could frighten the other most.

"Look! There's a hand!"

"Did you see that door close?"

"Something just crawled up that wall!" And the faintest sound, inside the house or out, would send them scurrying to the safety of their own yard.

In 1941 Don Chaffee was employed by Army Ordnance, and in 1942 he was transferred to Grand Rapids, Michigan, where he held a new position as Chief Inspector of Army

Ordnance at the Doehler-Jarvis plant. So in May, 1942, the Chaffees moved to Grand Rapids where the children were to finish their elementary and high school education. Roger was enrolled at Dickinson School and finished the remaining weeks of first grade there. Moving called for an adjustment in the lives of the Chaffee children. They made new friends easily, however and it was not long before they were both absorbed in their new surroundings.

2

Readin', Writin', 'n 'Rithmetic

"Is inclined to want to be the leader in games and free play but gives way quite gracefully upon my insistence. Is thoroughly dependable." These were the first words written on Roger's kindergarten report card. The same drive and determination to reach his goals, so clearcut in Roger's later life, were evident even in his first year of school.

In that same report the teacher made another prophetic entry: "Has a remarkable talent for hard work and use of tools. Is creative with wood, etc., far beyond anyone else in the group."

The last entry on the card was: "Tested up splendidly on both I.Q. test and reading readiness. Should do fine work next year." With this excellent record, six-year-old Roger Chaffee had completed his kindergarten work at Central Elementary School in Greenville.

At the time the children started school, they also developed an intense love for pets. Over the years they housed rabbits, dogs, birds, turtles and goldfish, and each new arrival was met with great enthusiasm and mountains of attention. As time went on, those mountains would shrink, however, and Mom and Dad would find themselves "keepers of the livestock" — a typical family situation.

The ending of the 1942 school year brought the beginning of Vacation Bible School. This was considered a good thing by the Chaffees, and they encouraged Roger's and Donna's attendance. It was almost the last pleasant thing about that first summer in Grand Rapids. No sooner had Bible School ended than Roger came down with the measles, and when he was nearly well, Donna took her turn. By the time they had both recovered fully, it was about time for school to begin again. The summer ended on a happy note, however. Arrangements had been made for Roger's first airplane ride. It was a family affair with Dad, Mom and Donna all sharing the experience.

The flight went out of the Grand Rapids airport, westward to Lake Michigan, about ten miles out over the water and then back to the airport — a short, but very meaningful ride! The excitement of the overwhelmed young man was indeed something to witness! That never-to-be-forgotten occasion salvaged that summer vacation from total loss for Roger.

Roger was now seven years old and ready for the second grade. At this age he was prone to severe throat problems, and this caused Don and Mike to be very strict about his wearing a hat and coat in cool weather. One windy March day Roger came home to lunch in tears. His hat had been thrown up into a tree by some older boys. Mom dried the tears understandingly; another cap was found and Roger returned to school, but a few days later Father brought home a small set of boxing gloves, and Roger was taught the fundamentals of boxing. He also was taught never to *start* a fight, but that he should not be afraid to stand up for what he thought was right. How many times he made use of this instruction no one knows, but he never came home with outward signs of battle. He seemed to develop the philosophy that disagreements were better talked about than fought about. Since talking was one of Roger's talents, this usually worked to his advantage.

All of Roger's school days were marked with characteristic hard work and the determination to succeed at his task. His grades reflected his drive and ambition although he was not what one would term a bookworm.

Weekends continued to be especially active for the family.

Sometimes they would visit the grandparents still living in Greenville; or, if the weather was nice, they might take a picnic supper to a park or a trip to the local zoo. If the weather did not lend itself to outings, the public museum or a suitable movie provided many hours of entertainment for the children. Whatever they did, however, they did as a family.

Tuesday evenings in the summertime the Chaffees followed a schedule that seldom varied; Ramona Amusement Park, with half-price rides for children, was their destination! The Chaffees made it a point to leave the house early in order to arrive at the park by 6:30 p.m., which was the time the fireman started the fire in the small locomotive that pulled the little passenger cars around the park, blowing its whistle at all the crossings. To take a ride on the train was a *must*, but to see the head of steam worked up and the little locomotive brought out of the roundhouse was that special "something else." Roger would stand with his nose pressed against the fence so firmly that rust spots would have to be wiped from his face before going any farther. He closely observed every action of the fireman until the whistle was sounded and the little train rolled along to the station to pick up its first passengers of the evening.

The Chaffees presented Roger with a Lionel electric train when he was about eight years old. He had had smaller trains previous to this time, but the Lionel was extra fine. Additional track, tunnels, stations, etc., were added from time to time as Christmas and birthday gifts, and the layout grew until it finally encircled the complete living room floor — under the davenport and chairs and around table legs. It eventually grew to such proportions that the whole family was needed to keep the train on the track! Sometimes even visiting friends or relatives joined in the fun. The enchanting sight of the miniature engine puffing smoke, its headlight gleaming in the early evening dusk was a fascination not only to Roger but to the adults as well!

Like most boys, Roger also liked guns. Over a period of time he had collected almost every conceivable type of toy gun, cannon, soldier and sailor. His first real BB gun was given to him when he was six years old. Prior to that time he had watched Grandfather Chaffee, an ardent gun lover, clean and care for his revolvers. Roger always enjoyed this immensely and would often ask his grandfather, "Don't you think it's time to clean the guns?" No one knows the many words of advice that Grandfather gave Roger regarding guns and their care, but from his future love for and knowledge of guns, it is certain that whatever Grandfather said, Roger accepted.

When Roger got his BB gun, he was taught to give it the fullest respect and was made to understand that *this* gun was not a toy. It was to be handled only when Dad or Grandfather was present. Often the two of them, or more often, the three of them, would head for the nearest gravel pit for a shooting spree. After each session the gun was cleaned and put away in the closet with as much care as the most expensive of rifles.

Another sport enjoyed by all the Chaffees was ice skating. One winter they made their own rink in the backyard. The whole family worked hard scraping away the snow, packing it down firmly, building a rim all around the area and then spraying it with the garden hose. Many times Don could be found re-spraying the pond at midnight so the children might find a smooth surface waiting for them the next day. Roger learned to skate on this backyard pond. After a considerable number of bumps and tumbles, he became a master of the blades and was allowed to go to the city parks on Saturday and Sunday afternoons. Until the children were old enough to go unattended, the family went to the larger rinks together.

Sports-minded as they were, the Chaffee's backyard was put to good use the year 'round — skating in the winter, badminton and croquet in the summer. There they also served free lunches to the squirrels that would come within a foot or two for the proffered snack.

Like all healthy boys, Roger enjoyed good food. Finding a dish of something he particularly disliked on the table, he sometimes would decide he was not nearly as hungry as he had thought, but Mike was firm. "No vegetable, no dessert," she would say. After eying the dish with distaste and weighing his dislike against his greed for delicious dessert, he would usually scoop an acceptable amount of the food in question onto his plate and chew rapidly.

His tactful charms made an early appearance in the kitchen. One day his mother was lamenting the condition of some of her cooking utensils, and he, boyishly loyal, said, "Don't you worry about that, Mom. The food tastes good anyway!"

At an early age Roger was given a small allowance to help teach him the value of money; he was also given his own bank into which his savings were deposited. As he grew older the allowance was increased, with some stipulations, however. He was permitted to use his allowance for anything he wanted, provided his savings deposit was made first. When his weekly allowance was gone, there was no more to be had until the following week. During the years of World War II war stamps and bonds were almost compulsory. Roger invested part of his allowance in these United States Savings Stamps at school and accumulated two or three bonds in this way.

When Donna and Roger began their later elementary school years, their parents began attaching provisions to the allowances. "No work, no allowance," was their philosophy. The young people soon got the message and became busily involved in household tasks.

One of these was the most tedious of household chores, the "dish detail." After some bickering the children agreed between themselves that Roger would wash and Donna would dry. Everything would move along smoothly until Donna discovered a spot on a dish she was drying. Then the battle would blaze as she tried to return the dish to Roger for rewashing, while he loudly insisted that getting those spots off was the wiper's job!

The final battle always ensued after the dishes were done with Donna insisting it was the washer's job to clean the sink. Roger loudly proclaimed that he was the *washer*, and the *washer* only, and when finished washing, *he* was through. When the battle grew so fierce that the dishes rattled in reverberation, their parents intervened in self-defense. Donna laughingly recalls now that she usually cleaned the sink!

Donna also recalls a few other experiences concerning Roger:

One day she caught Roger and his friend sitting behind the chicken coop smoking corn silk in corn cob pipes. They both looked pretty sick, and when Roger pleaded with her not to tell Mom or Dad, she agreed. He didn't forget the lesson he learned that day and never smoked again. Sometimes he did learn the hard way. One Christmas he drank the juice from a bottle of olives and became very ill.

Every Christmas season the Chaffees would talk the children

27

into taking some of their toys to the fire department as gifts for other children. They were difficult to convince at times, but they knew they would be getting new toys when Santa came. Neither had doubts as to who Santa was!

Sometimes in the summer, when time hung heavily on their hands, the children would get a fruit jar and catch bees from the flower garden and then drown them in a pail of water. They could not explain afterward why they did this. Perhaps it was Roger's way of wreaking vengeance for the sting on his nose! Actually Roger was not a mean boy; he usually was considerate of animals as well as people.

In the fourth grade Roger learned to swim. Because of the many family jaunts around Grand Rapids, he felt confident he could find his way about. He was allowed to join the YMCA and each week took the bus to his swimming class.

His interest in music developed in the fifth grade. After a voice test he was selected to participate in a city-wide choral group which practiced and presented their programs at the Park Congregational Church, one of Grand Rapids' largest churches. He also joined the school band and in a remarkably short time learned to play the French horn. After conquering this difficult instrument, he decided that the cornet was much more glamorous and requested permission to make the change. The French horn was loaned to him by the school, but after proving he could make the transition, he received a used cornet from his family. This was his very own, and he took much pride in it, keeping the horn in excellent condition for the two years he used it. His progress was so good that when he entered junior high school, he was given a brand new trumpet.

During one Easter vacation Roger was the cause of a good deal of excitement. His grandparents were visiting for the holiday, and Mike had prepared a special Good Friday night supper of fried smelt. Later that evening Roger complained of severe stomach ache and soreness, and since smelt was one of his favorite dishes and he had eaten a substantial quantity, the family teased him playfully about the painful results of over-eating. But as the evening wore on and he continued to feel ill, Mike called the doctor who ordered him into Butterworth Hospital for additional diagnosis. The results of the tests sent Roger into surgery for an appendectomy at 11:00 p.m., that same night. The operation went well, however, and although that Easter Sunday was spent in the hospital, it was not long before he was able to return home, ready and eager to involve himself in his multitudes of projects and activities. For Roger with his many interests, life was always exciting.

Almost any activity of an outdoor nature was appealing to Roger. He inherited the family love for fishing and was thrilled on one particular quest for lake trout in Grand Traverse Bay, when he was allowed to fish off the stern of the boat, sitting in a fishing chair, using a heavy rod with copper wire line. This was quite a combination for a young lad to handle, but he manfully measured up to the job and took his turn in the chair. His enthusiasm was a treat to see, and even Mom and Donna became excited as they watched the drag on his line and examined his more than acceptable "catch."

About once a year the family usually made a trip to Canada to visit relatives. Roger and Donna looked forward to those trips because, in addition to the pleasure of seeing their uncle and aunt, they visited so many interesting places on the way. They were especially thrilled with the opportunity to put on boots, hats and raincoats and go under the Niagara Falls. Returning from Canada they sometimes stopped in Detroit to spend a day at the zoo. Though they never saw the train there work up its steam, they usually rode it half way around the park and then leisurely walked back, taking in all the points of interest. During the war years, there was only one Canada trip, due to the rigid gas rationing in effect. However, by saving stamps and limiting other unnecessary trips, they were able to squeeze one such excursion into that period.

Birthdays at the Chaffee home were usually celebrated at the evening meal, which was the best time for all the family to assemble with leisure. On Roger's twelfth birthday he was given a twenty-two repeating rifle. His mother had fixed on excellent dinner, including most of Roger's favorite foods and a special cake. However, on this occasion at least, he was so overwhelmed with his newest possession that he was hardly aware of what he ate. He hurried through his mother's carefully planned dinner and excused himself to go off to the firing range to try out his gift. To a boy with Roger's love of guns, the new rifle was unutterable joy.

Soon after this he decided to take a route for the *Grand Rapids Herald,* a morning paper, and plunged into the routine with much enthusiasm. By 5:00 a.m., he would be off and many times be back again for a short nap before the rest of the family was up and about for breakfast. As with so many projects, one thing seemed to call for another, and Roger's paper route seemed to demand a bicycle. An agreement was made with a local merchant allowing Roger to pay two dollars weekly out of his earnings. The cost of the bike was $48, an amount that must have loomed large to a twelve-year-old boy, but he never missed a payment.

On Sundays, when the paper was especially large, Dad drove Roger around the route in the family car, passing the papers out the window to be thrown onto the porches. Roger Chaffee was not the cartoon caricature of the paper boy, for his aim was accurate, and he was conscientious about getting the papers *on* the porches. Elderly customers became accustomed to finding their papers helpfully tucked inside the screen door.

One elderly neighbor lady was much impressed with Roger's thoughtfulness and came to depend on him for many things. She put him to work shopping for her, taking out trash, shoveling sidewalks and doing many other odd jobs. On one occasion she had him replace a broken basement window, and even though he was only twelve years old, he knew exactly how it was done. Just previously he had broken one of the Chaffee windows with a ball, and Father had explained the procedure perfectly! Circumstances differed, however, in that he was paid for replacing her window but had to pay Father for his.

This same dear lady was once the source of real embarrassment to Roger. As he was leaving her home one day, he asked politely if there was anything else he could do for her. "Yes," she said, "there *is* one more thing." She was in need of some hosiery. Would he buy them for her? Roger gulped but courteously promised that he would. At this unprecedented request even *his* gentlemanly nature rebelled. He shuddered inwardly at the thought of going into a store to ask for the heavy silk hose desired. Mike came to the rescue, however, and purchased the stockings for him.

It was not long before the enterprising Roger discovered an added source of income. His paper route took him over a large area, and he observed how hard it was to find the house numbers of some of his customers. He decided he could paint the numbers on the risers of the homeowners' front steps — for a price, of course. First, he built a box out of some lumber scraps to carry his supplies; then, with a little financial assistance from Dad and Mom, he bought paint and brushes, and Dad had the stencils cut at the shop. Then Roger canvassed the area and found without surprise that this was a paying enterprise, a dollar for each job. Many people used his services, and Roger became a real "young businessman."

11801

Roger's early years, from sandbox to Purdue University. Girl in pictures, Roger's sister, Donna. Gentleman in fishing picture is Grandfather Chaffee.

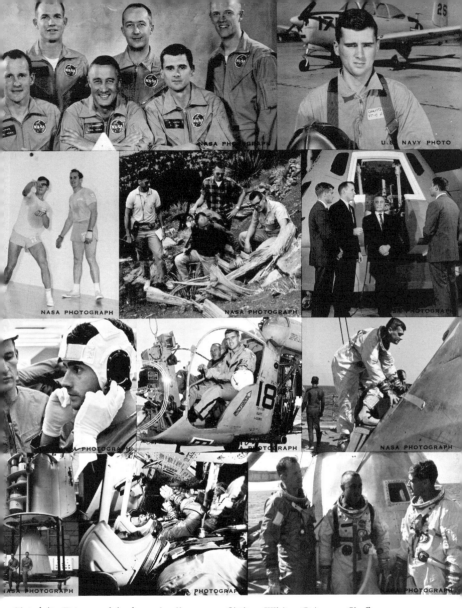

Top left: Prime and back-up Apollo crews. *Sitting,* White, Grissom, Chaffee; *standing:* L-R, David Scott, Jim McDivitt and Rusty Schweickart. *Top right:* Roger after completing first solo, June, 1958. *2nd row:* L-R, Chaffee & White in private gym at Cape Kennedy; *Center:* Field training, Chaffee, Scott, Bean & instructor; *Right:* Engineer from North American Aviation (extreme right) interviewing Apollo crew. *3rd row:* L. White and Chaffee check equipment; *Center,* Chaffee, Helicopter training; R. Chaffee inspecting Command Module during water egress training. *Bottom:* Crew members in front of full scale mock-up of space vehicle's Service Module; *Center,* Crew with mock-up of actual control panel; *Right,* Crew suited up on deck of *Retriever.*

Top left: Action shot of water egress training; *Right,* Roger watches spacecraft components being worked on at North American Aviation plant, Downey, California. *Center row,* left: Roger during helicopter training, Pensacola, Fla. *Top right:* Roger serving as communications officer for a Gemini flight. *Bottom right:* Classic Chaffee pose struck during an interview. *Bottom row,* left: Roger and Martha, at presentation of Air Medal by NASA's Dr. Gilruth; *right:* Apollo equipment check, North American Aviation, Downey, Calif.

Top, left: Paul Haney, Public Affairs Officer, Manned Spacecraft Center at press conference, detailing deaths of Apollo crew. (Emotion & sorrow of moment are obvious.); *Right:* Still wearing flight suit, Astronaut Frank Borman hurries to offer condolences to the Chaffee family. *Bottom left:* Astronauts give a pilot's tribute as 3 jets streak through the sky, leaving empty slot for their comrade. Westminster Presbyterian Church, near Houston, day of funeral. *Bottom, right:* President Johnson offers condolences to Martha Chaffee at Arlington. Astronaut Eugene Cernan in background.

37

NASA PHOTO

Top: Six horses, three riderless, draw caisson toward gravesite in Arlington National Cemetery; *Bottom:* Crack Naval honor guard prepares to fold flag above casket of Roger Chaffee. Arlington National Cemetery.

Top: Astronaut Eugene Cernan tries to console Stephen Chaffee, 5, at burial services for father. Mother and sister look on, while grandparents, Mr. and Mrs. Donald Chaffee and President Lyndon B. Johnson bow their heads in grief. *Bottom:* Martha Chaffee accepts for Roger the NASA posthumous award, the Exceptional Service Medal, October 23, 1967.

NASA PHOTOGRAPH

IN LIVING MEMORY TO
ROGER B. CHAFFEE
LT. COMDR – U.S. NAVY
ASTRONAUT – APOLLO 1

MAY HIS DEDICATION
BE OUR INSPIRATION

PRESENTED 7 MAY 1967 BY THE
NASSAU BAY GARDEN CLUB

GRAND RAPIDS PRESS PHOTO

GRAND RAPIDS PRESS PH

Top: Dedication of Christmas tree presented by Nassau Bay Garden Club of Houston. Stephen and Sheryl unveil plaque. (Insert overlay) close-up of plaque; *Bottom, left:* Astronaut Eugene Cernan at dedication of Roger B. Chaffee Memorial Planetarium in Grand Rapids, Michigan. Chaffee's parents sit on platform in background. *Grand Rapids Press* photograph. *Right:* Mr. and Mrs. Donald Chaffee accept Liberty Bell Award presented by Grand Rapids Bar Association, May, 1967. *Grand Rapids Press.*

3

The Good Scout

It was during Roger's junior and senior years at Central High School that the Boy Scout organization played such an important role in his life. With his varied interests and unending curiosity, Roger was the personification of the "all around boy." He earned his first merit badge at the age of thirteen. During that year, 1948, he earned a total of ten merit badges, an unusual accomplishment.

His first badges, earned in February, were for Home Repairs and Firemanship. In March he was given the Personal Health Badge. April of that same year brought him the Safety, Athletic, and Public Health Awards. The Athletic Award involved field events such as the high jump and broad jump and was difficult for a thirteen-year-old boy to attain. Winning the Safety Award involved not only bicycle and auto safety but also the setting up of a fire escape system for his home. It was more than a little unusual for a boy of Roger's age to win the Safety Award. The Swimming, First Aid and Cooking Badges were received in November, though the Swimming Award usually was earned by boys in the fourteen to sixteen age bracket. Roger's trips to the YMCA were beginning to pay off! His last award in 1948 was the Order of the Arrow which is a Camper Society Award and usually reserved for boys fifteen or older. This was an exceptionally great honor for Roger.

During the following year of 1949 when Roger was fourteen years old, he received four merit badges, Scholarship, Rowing, Life-Saving and Canoeing. Again he had achieved the unusual by attaining these awards at such a young age.

In 1950 Roger, now fifteen, continued to demonstrate his interest and ability in scouting. He won the Pathfinder, Pioneering, Music and Seamanship Merit Badges. The Seamanship Award was especially difficult because, among other things, its achievement required the ability to pilot a sailboat.

By the time Roger had completed the eleventh grade, he had earned just about all the merit badges available to Boy Scouts at that time. That year he received the badges for Camping, Civics, Bird Study and Bugling and was eligible to become an Eagle Scout, a coveted achievement. During the Eagle Scout ceremony, after Roger had received his pin, the director presented a miniature Eagle emblem to Roger's mother. It remains one of her most valued possessions, a symbol of an important steppingstone in her boy's life.

The last Boy Scout awards that Roger received were the Bronze and Gold Palms. The Gold Palm was presented to him in 1953 and signified that Roger had earned ten additional merit badges after becoming an Eagle Scout.

Roger loved children and was always helpful to the younger Scouts. He spent one summer at Camp Shawondossee, just north of Muskegon, Michigan, as Assistant Water-Front Director, teaching these younger Scouts to swim. His Boy Scout leader later revealed that Roger would have received his Eagle Scout rating at an even earlier age than sixteen, but he spent so much time helping younger Scouts that he did not have time to finish his own qualifications. This selflessness was typical of Roger Chaffee.

The scouting years were busy ones for the whole Chaffee family. Honor award dinners, family Scout picnics, cookouts and, of course, weekend camping trips were all attended regularly. It seemed that whenever a camping trip was planned, Roger somehow managed to get on the food committee! Consequently, the Chaffees spent countless hours at the kitchen table deciding on various menus and figuring just how much food a group of growing boys would devour on a weekend in the out-of-doors. They determined how many cups of flour, shortening, milk, carrots, onions and beef were required for Roger's favorite dish, beef stew and dumplings, and this became a regular patrol meal. The Eagle Patrol was never known to go hungry on any of its camping trips.

Over the years Roger became a very good cook in his own right and was always willing to experiment with new dishes. He loved outdoor-barbecuing and was a master chef at the grill. There was never any danger of his going hungry, as he could always find something from which to make a meal.

Summer meant Scout Camp for Roger. He financed these excursions by taking a portion of his weekly allowance and depositing it with the troop on meeting nights. Scouting clothes and equipment were acquired over the years as Christmas and birthday gifts from the family.

Though his scouting interests consumed a good deal of time, Roger was an excellent student in school and spent much time preparing lessons. In the eighth grade he wrote the following prophetic theme:

"Why I Chose My Career"

I would like to be an electronics engineer.

I am 14 years old. I was born February 15, 1935. I am in good health except I am a little on the heavy side.

I have a good family life except my sister is two years older than I am and she thinks she can boss me. I have certain chores to do and I get a good allowance.

My parents say I can do and be what I want to. I want to be an electronics engineer or a radio technician. Ever since I was old enough to know what electricity does, it has fascinated me. As of now, I am pretty much interested in radio for I am reading a few radio books and making a radio.

I can work with electricity and radio best because I like it; if I don't like something, I can't do it. At home I build radios. I am now building a short wave radio and helping a friend with one.

At school I am best in arithmetic, for I like to work with figures.

I'm in the Scouts and am a member of Troop 215. I have the rank of Star Scout and I am a patrol leader.

For friends I like to have kids who will stick up for their own rights. I don't like girls and boys who are intolerant. I don't care for the ones that go home if they can't have their own way.

I admire a person with a clean mind, one that has the ambition to make something of himself, that does his work without crabbing. I also very much admire a good sport.

I chose electronics as I have said before, because I have always liked to play with motors. I also like to play with and make radios. I feel that I can succeed because I like the subject, and I think that if you like the subject enough and if you try hard enough that you can succeed, and I will certainly try. I also think that it would be a fascinating subject to study in college. It is still a subject in which you have an opportunity to really go a long way and that's what I like.

One only has to know that Roger's scholastic average during his high school years was better than 92 per cent to recognize that he did indeed strive to do well in school. On September 26, 1951, Roger took the Kuder Vocational Tests, scoring highest in Scientifics. He also scored very high in Mechanical and Artistic — a surprise to no one. Already he was on his way to becoming the scientist he wanted to be.

Roger's interest in science continued to grow, and at about the age of fifteen he developed a yearning to have his own workshop and laboratory. Since the family had just converted the heating system in their home from coal to gas, he requested permission to transform the old coal bin into a workroom for his own use. His parents readily agreed to his use of the room, and out came the broom, soap and hot water. He scrubbed and rinsed over and over again until satisfied that the bin was ready for white wash. When all was completed, his reward for the hard work was an unfinished desk for his new work area.

One winter evening shortly after, Roger went to the workshop to experiment with his chemistry set. Suddenly, he came dashing up the stairs, the pungent smell of burnt sulphur following close behind. Windows and doors were thrown open, and Don Chaffee delivered an oration on the necessity for following the directions in the chemistry manual!

Roger's interest in chemistry continued into his high school years even though he also developed many new interests. His paper route fell by the wayside as academic and sports activities grew more numerous. He enjoyed football and went out for the team every season. Although he never became a star player, he did play enough to qualify for a letter at the season's end.

Roger continued with his trumpet even though he could not play football and be in the band at the same time. He and several other boys formed a small dance band which was well received, and they played for the after-game dances for a small fee. This arrangement allowed him to play the game and his horn too.

Model airplanes, then becoming very complicated, continued to claim a share of his time throughout high school. Motors, gas tanks, wire line and U-Reeley reels were then in vogue. It was the power age with planes of all sizes and shapes being created. At one time eight models hung from Roger's bedroom ceiling. For years flying these planes was a family affair in which even Grandmother and Grandfather took part when visiting on weekends. Two or three of the planes would be put into the trunk of the car, and away they would go to a local park where there was plenty of room to fly the models. The whole family enjoyed the spectacle, excited and happy when the planes were flying right or sorry and disappointed when they crashed. "Oh well," Roger would say, "one more repair job coming up."

At sixteen Roger was a handsome, athletic boy with brown, wavy hair. Like most boys of that age, he was eager to learn to drive, and he prevailed upon his father to teach him. This was no time-consuming job for the self-confident, mechanically minded young man, and he was soon awarded a driver's license. He was then allowed to use the family car on occasion, but it was not long before he set his sights on owning a car of his own — an ambition resulting in considerable family discussion. Obtaining the desired car required some fast talking by Roger. Although Roger had been no trouble to the Chaffees — over and above the usual family differences of opinion — he was always ready to argue at the drop of a hat. Now there were many after-dinner discussions held in which Roger would take the opposite side just for the sake of argument and was always convincing, even when the others knew he was wrong.

But a car!

Finally, after much persuasion, he obtained parental consent and after shopping around, discovered a real "prize." His faithful old bicycle was sold for twenty-five dollars, and he took an additional twenty-four dollars from his savings, purchasing a 1929 Lafayette for forty-nine dollars. It was strictly a "fun car," but it took him where he wanted to go. In a few months he discovered another "prize" — a 1934 Ford Sport Coupe. This car was priced at $125. Being one to drive a hard bargain, Roger was able to get sixty-five dollars for the Lafayette and charged the balance due on the Ford. He now had a real jalopy that he was proud to drive back and forth to Scout Camp at Duck Lake, his earnings at the camp paying the balance on the car.

Roger also earned money working in the Boy Scout Department of Herpolsheimer's Department Store. He was very proud of his job and handled it with outstanding ability. He became friends with his department head at the store, and shortly after being appointed an astronaut in 1963, he wrote the following letter to the eight-year-old son of the man who had been his boss:

Dear Steven:

It might take me a few days to get around to it, but I always have time to answer letters to a nice little gentleman like you.

This is especially true when they are sons of old friends of mine. Yes, when I was in high school and a Boy Scout in Grand Rapids I worked for your father in Herpolsheimer's boys' department. That was the first real job I ever had.

You asked me to tell you how I became an astronaut. It is a long story that involves many people but I will try to tell you some of it. I might say some things that you won't understand completely, but your dad can explain them to you, and when you are a little older, you'll be able to understand how important they are.

First of all, you have to *want* to be an astronaut. That means you want to be a jet pilot and an engineer and you have to want to do things that are exciting and challenging like riding on a roller coaster or going down the biggest hill there is, on a sled.

These things you can understand, but there are far more important things. You have to want to dedicate your life to a worthwhile cause and to serve your country. You have to love your country so much that every time you see our flag you feel warm inside.

Secondly, you must always challenge your ability while you are growing. You must be given and assume the responsibilities you can handle. This is where your father helped me so much.

When I came to work for him at Herpolsheimer's, he gave me the responsibility of the Boy Scout department. It made me feel important and gave me the knowledge that I could stand on my own two feet. For you at your age, this means that you should take the chores that your mother and father give you around the house and do them better than they have ever been done before. And then when you are older, you will be given bigger jobs with more responsibility because you have proved you can do any job given you.

The third thing you must do to become an astronaut is to study very hard. I know you study real hard, Steve, because of the fine letter you wrote me. The words and the sentences were good, and the handwriting was excellent for the second grade. I have a son named Steve and he is two years old. I hope he can write letters that nice when he is eight.

You always have to study hard, in grade school, high school and college. I am still studying and I will keep on studying all the time I am an astronaut. There are other things besides school that have to be studied. There is your church or Sunday School, and when you get a little older, there are the Cub Scouts and the Boy Scouts. Scouting is a lot of fun and you learn a lot of things that come in handy to jet pilots and astronauts.

Another thing you have to do to become an astronaut is to keep your body strong by playing outdoor games like baseball and basketball, football, running and swimming. Keeping your body strong also helps you keep your mind strong so you can study better.

And then, Steve, if you have done a good job on all of these things and have graduated from college, you can learn to fly the big jet airplanes in the Air Force or Navy. And after you have flown them for about six years and have proved that you can do the jobs given you, you can try for astronaut training.

It sounds like an awful lot for an eight-year-old to do and

think about it, doesn't it, Steve? But if you always do your best and ask your mother and father and your teachers, they can tell you what to do next if you want to become an astronaut or anything else.

Thank you very much for your fine letter.

Sincerely,

Roger B. Chaffee

Like most teen-age boys, Roger enjoyed tinkering with a car. He once spent one whole weekend cleaning the motor of his with gasoline and painting the area under the hood with aluminum paint. Justly proud of the results of his efforts, he got a real kick out of having people lift the hood and find everything inside so shiny bright. One had only to look at Roger's car to know it was his pride and joy.

One evening he drove his car to the high school for a basketball game and afterwards found that someone had cut three long slashes in the top of his precious Ford. That cut *him* too. He could not imagine anyone being so destructive and unkind.

Roger did some dating while in high school, and one of these friends referred to his car in a recent letter to the Chaffees:

> Maybe you remember when Roger had that old "antique now" car that he did not realize was without a jack until we had a flat tire. Then he tried to decide which house he could go to where the people wouldn't mind his pounding on the door after 11:00 p.m., to ask for a jack to borrow. Fortunately, the first house he chose had a good natured occupant.

She also reminisced about another time during their high school years:

> My thoughts reflect back to a day in Roger's senior year when we were sitting together in the back of the school auditorium discussing everything from our math problems to our philosophies of life. It was at that time that I remember him saying, "I'm not going to college just to earn a degree; I'm going to really make something of myself." Little did I realize then the full impact of those words. However, ten years later I couldn't help but say to myself — "Well, Rog, you certainly did do that!"

Roger found time for other serious thinking, too, about things like life — and death. Another time, after attending a movie in which there was a funeral scene, he remarked to his friend, "A funeral should be a happier occasion than a wedding." Roger did not fear death.

Roger kept his car until just before leaving home for college. One day a stranger passing by the house saw the car with its "For Sale" sign. He was looking for an old car body in good condition that he could "soup up" with a heavy motor for racing, and since he felt this car would more than meet his need, he offered Roger $250 for it. Seeing a golden opportunity to double his investment, Roger sold. He was more than a little pleased with his profit as a car dealer.

In the eleventh grade Roger wrote the following theme which showed his sincere and continuing determination to make his mark in the scientific field:

"My Vocation In Nuclear Physics"

I have chosen for my vocation nuclear physics. Nuclear physics is a specialized branch of physics dealing with atomic energy. In this branch I would be primarily engaged in research for the Atomic Energy Commission or teaching in some school where there would be a chance for research. I would be surrounded by men of high mental capacity. I would work in a clean place such as any other lab and have pleasant people and personalities around me. There are practically no physical hazards outside of the usual chance of burned hands and fingers except maybe one chance in a thousand of radiation poisoning and burns. But there are mental hazards. There is a great strain on the mind; a physicist can't forget his problems. When he goes home at night he just takes them with him.

My personal qualifications are fair for this field. I rated highest on my "Kuder" test in science and math. I have always been interested in science since I got a chemistry set when I was about eight years old. I am also very interested in mechanics and aeronautics. I would like very much to become a scientist in some other field if I could not make the grade in nuclear physics. My parents' desire for me is pretty much the same as mine. They say that they will help me become anything I wish, but they distinctly want to have me go to college if at all possible.

I think my personality and temperament are fairly well suited to this kind of job. A person in this field should have a scientific aptitude. I believe I have one. He should have an adaptability and interest in what he is doing; I am always interested in science. He should be patient. Sometimes I become a little hasty, but most of the time I can control myself. I am inclined to be a little on the bull-headed side which would not be in the best interests for landing a job. When I am tired I am apt to be a little hot tempered, but I might grow out of this with age and education. I am very gregarious which is good, for a scientist is always among people.

My abilities for this job are good. Academically I'm fitted for science. My best marks are in math and science. They always have been. I also am high in mechanical drawing. In school, about the only subjects I enjoy are math and chemistry. For special abilities and skills I am fairly good in mechanical things, working on cars, doing electric work, and things like that. I can play a trumpet fairly well and play in a dance band. None of these things have much to do with physics, but everyone in order to work well should have a hobby or something to take his mind off of his work.

In some respects I think this is the job for me, and in others I don't. The arguments for it are I like math and I like to do work involving math. I also like chemistry and physics and thoroughly enjoy working with them. I think I could work fairly well with the type of people in that field, and the wages would suit me fine. But there are some points I am dubious on. First I like to work with my hands on mechanical things, and I don't know that if I was in this field I would have enough time outside of work to satisfy my desires. Second, I am sometimes inclined to be a little hot-tempered with people that try to tell me what to do. I hate to be ordered! Third, as of now I don't have the financial resources necessary to attend that kind of college, and for the length of time that I would have to go, still there is always a chance to win scholarships. All in all I believe I have about a fifty-fifty chance to achieve my goal if the army doesn't get me first.

There were, of course, several girls in the life of the handsome Roger. One young lady said later about him:

I met Roger while a senior in high school. The Roger Chaffee I knew was, as the term implies, "An All-American Boy." While in college I wrote a theme about Roger entitled, "Joe College." He was all of that, too. Everything he did, he did with perfection in mind. The goals that he set for himself in life reflected this attribute. In everything he did, perfection was called for, from teaching life-saving and sailing at Boy Scout Camp to landing an aircraft on a carrier.

Roger had a free-thinking, progressive and liberal mind. He very definitely was a modern man, but I cannot say he did not have any old-fashioned ideas. Where marriage was concerned he said he did not want his wife to work after marriage because he felt a wife's place was in the home.

Once, she said, they were involved in an accident with his father's car. It was not a serious accident, but it did damage the front of the car, and she received a bump on her head which caused a slight headache. The somewhat trivial accident, she said, caused tears to flow on Roger's part mainly because people he cared about were injured in one way or another, her head and his father's pocketbook.

Roger and Donna had attended Central High School together until Donna graduated and went on to junior college. Even in the closest of families, there comes a time of partial separation. So, with Donna's marriage in the early 1950's, Roger and Donna saw much less of each other. Each was now engrossed in his own pursuits, Donna that of housewife and mother, and Roger intent on his self-appointed course . . . a course to the stars.

It was now Roger's turn to graduate, and during his senior year he had much to do. He took tests, summarized class grades and applied for scholarships. He applied for three: Annapolis, Rhodes and Naval Reserve Officers Training Corps (NROTC).

He was in line for the appointment to Annapolis but summed up his feelings regarding *that* opportunity when he told his parents, "They wanted me to promise that if this is given to me, I will always remain in the Navy, and today I couldn't promise. I just don't know, and I don't want to lie about it."

Rhodes accepted his school grades, but because they did not accept applicants for engineering fields, he was eliminated. A few days before graduation day, word came that he had been accepted into the NROTC and was to report to the Illinois Institute of Technology in September of 1953.

Roger graduated from Grand Rapids Central High School on June 11, 1953, finishing in the top one-fifth of his class with almost all A's and B's. His impressive record was noted in the 1953 year book, *The Helios*:

> Football: 1, 2, 3, 4; Track: 1-2; "C" Club: 4; Hi-Y: 4; Math Club: 3, 4; Variety Show: 1, 3, 4; Senior Play Ticket Committee, 4; Dance Band: 2, 3, 4; Variety Show Ticket Committee: 4; March of Dimes: 4; Junior Potluck Committee: 3; Spring Concert: 1, 2, 3, 4; Senior Potluck Entertainment Committee: 4; Junior Play Entertainment: 3; Hy-Y Program Committee: 4; Big Brother-Big Sister: 4.

An enviable accumulation!

A former classmate from Central summed up Roger's high school days with the following words: "As I remember Rog in high school, I remember a well-balanced, mild-mannered friend who always managed to pull down good marks."

4

Joe College

Those fun-filled high school days were over. Now it was summer, and while waiting to begin his first term at the Illinois Institute of Technology, Roger worked in the Blue Print Room at the Lear plant in Grand Rapids. He enjoyed the work there and made many new friends.

The family spent long hours that summer discussing Roger's college plans. Although the older Chaffee's had reservations about his acceptance of the Naval scholarship, they realized that with the Korean conflict still unsettled, Roger, in excellent physical and mental condition, would surely be drafted anyway. (The truce came July 27th, but by that time, the decision was firm.) Since his choice was the Navy, they finally agreed that the NROTC program would be best for him. Roger made up his mind at that time to accept the program wholeheartedly and to take advantage of every opportunity it afforded.

There were a few boyhood bridges to be burned before leaving for college. He already had sold the jalopy, but there remained all his model airplanes and their equipment. Roger realized that there would be no time for these things once he entered college and let it be known that he was ready to sell. News traveled by word of mouth that there were some valuable airplanes and equipment for sale, and soon an interested party appeared. Roger sold out — all airplanes, repair equipment, reels, motors, tanks, fuel and tools for the grand amount of twenty-five dollars — a mere fraction of their worth. The buyer was a young married man with two small sons.

Summer was soon over and foot locker, garment bags and suitcases were packed into the car as the family accompanied Roger to Chicago to see him enrolled in college.

Loving mothers shed many tears over their children, and Mike Chaffee was indeed a loving mother. She had cried when she sent him off alone on the bus for his first swimming lesson; she cried when they left him for the first time at Boy Scout Camp. Now she wept again as they drove away from Chicago leaving Roger behind — a college freshman. He was entering a new life, one which the family could not enter with him. Realizing this, Don's eyes, too, were misty. They recognized that their son was now a man in a man's world and must make his own way.

During the first three weeks of school he took residence in the men's hall. Then came rush week. By the end of the month Roger informed his family that he was pledging the Phi Kappa Sigma Fraternity and moving into their house. Always warm and friendly, Roger quickly fell into step with his fraternity brothers, and one, Al Moreen, became a special buddy.

It was not possible for Roger to get home from Chicago very often, but when he did he was usually accompanied by two or three other students whose homes were farther away. Even some of the hometown Chicago men came to Grand Rapids with him for weekend visits. No matter how many appeared at the house, the Chaffees found room for them and enjoyed hearing about the antics of "fraternity men."

Roger's first year in college was routine as far as studies were concerned. His name appeared on the Dean's List of Undergraduate Honor Students, and he finished the first year carrying a B+ average. By the time summer vacation had rolled around he had made a definite decision to follow a career in aeronautical engineering. This decision actually came as a surprise to no one who knew him.

Even as a senior in high school, he had had some very definite ideas about what he wanted out of life and where he was going. Like an actor who strives to see his name in lights, Roger had said he wanted his to be in the history books. He had told friends he wanted to be the first man on the moon. The amazing part about this was that it was not until about four years later that Russia put their Sputnik in space. Either Roger even then was very well read on the subject of space and interplanetary travel, or he had such a progressive mind that he could foresee the "Space Age" as it is now called, as a fact of the future. Even as a boy, his favorite character was Buck Rogers!

That summer of 1954 he was to take his first summer cruise in accordance with the NROTC program. Before qualifying for this it was necessary for him to undergo additional training and physical tests at Great Lakes Naval Training Station. This examination very nearly eliminated him from his career in aviation. The eye examination came late in the afternoon of an exceedingly tiring day, and one eye was so weak that the doctor thought seriously of failing him in this test. Before doing so, however, he told Roger to come back the next morning after a good night's rest and try again.

Before going to bed that night Roger spent some time walking along the Lake Michigan beach, thinking. If he failed the eye test the next morning, he knew that flying for the Navy would be out. Failure was not acceptable! He was determined to pass it and later told of his many prayers that night. The next morning he *did* pass the test. He had climbed yet another step further "on course."

The first summer cruise lasted eight weeks aboard the Battleship *Wisconsin*. He was always thoughtful of the folks back home and kept them well posted on all his trips around the U.S.A., and the world. They received cards and letters from almost every port he visited, and upon returning home to Grand Rapids, he brought to each of the family some memento typical of the various countries visited. During that first summer cruise he visited England; Glasgow, Scotland; Paris, France; and Cuba.

After Roger returned from the training cruise, his father found him a job with Gear Research, working in the shop. It was a very dirty job, running an automatic gear-cutter on soft black iron material, and each day he came out at the end of his shift looking like a coal miner. Roger disliked being dirty, but he worked hard anyway and at the end of those weeks commented, "I learned one thing on this job. I'm not going to make my living *this* way for the rest of my life!"

Roger came from a line of hard workers. His lineage dated back to 1635 in America and beyond that in England. None of his ancestors had been born with the proverbial silver spoon; the Chaffees earned what they had. But though Roger was willing to work hard, if there was an easier way to accomplish a job, he set about to find it.

When Roger decided definitely to become an aeronautical engineer, he made application for transfer to Purdue University in order to take advantage of the excellent program offered there. This transfer was sanctioned by the review board in Washington.

September, 1954, found the Chaffee household in another state of inventory-taking and the foot locker in use once again. Roger's belongings were again loaded into the family car, and they set off for Purdue University in Lafayette, Indiana.

Entering the town of Lafayette, they went directly to 234 Littleton Street, West Lafayette, which was to be Roger's fraternity home for the next three years. A letter of introduction from his fraternity brothers in Chicago had preceded him, and members of the Lafayette fraternity were waiting for him. It was a warm welcome to the University.

Roger went home occasionally when he could hitch a ride north. He would write frequently, however, and also was allowed to call home "collect" as often as he felt the need. The calls were worth much more to Don and Mike than the price of the phone bill, as they could usually tell by his voice if all was well.

After the routine of classes and studies was established, Chaffee looked for part-time work to augment the monthly check from home. His first job at Purdue was waiting on tables in one of the women's halls. Though this sounded to his fraternity brothers like an enviable position, the solely feminine atmosphere was not to Roger's liking, and he began to look around for something else. He found a nice position with a small concern in West Lafayette doing drafting for a few hours each week. This work he enjoyed and remained with the firm on a part-time basis through his sophomore year.

It was Roger's ambition to get as much out of college as was possible. Science and mathematics continued to be favorite subjects. He wanted to work extra subjects into his schedule and in 1955 decided to take a summer school session. Since this would interfere with his Naval program, it was arranged for him to make up this phase of training at the end of his college years.

During Roger's sophomore and junior years at Purdue, his parents visited him on two special occasions: Mother's Day in the spring and a Father's Day celebration in the fall. These events were campus-wide, but their main concern was with the activities of the Phi Kappa Sigma Fraternity House.

The mothers of the boys in the house had organized a Mother's Club, and on Mother's Day they had their annual meeting. The fathers also were invited for those weekends. The families brought food from home, and the Saturday evening dinner was smorgasbord style. The grand rush for the serving line when the fellows laid eyes on all that longed-for home cooking was a rare sight!

At bedtime the fathers were escorted to the second story of the house to sleep on whatever was convenient — chairs, tables, desk tops and even the floor in the various study rooms. The mothers were taken to the third floor and each assigned to her son's bunk.

The bunk beds were stacked three high, with not more than two feet of aisle space between the rows. The laughing and joking mothers could be heard throughout the house as these "staid, dignified" women attempted to crawl into the top layer of bunks. The good time was considered well worth any loss of dignity.

The ladies were scarcely settled, however, when the sound of singing came from below. They scrambled out of their hard-won positions and huddled around the front dormer window. A bright spotlight from the roof revealed their sons, grouped in a semi-circle in the front yard, their young voices rising on the soft midnight breeze and blending in the harmony of "Ivy Halls" and the "Whiffenpoof Song." Their last rendition was a parody of "Good Night, Ladies," the closing lines changed to "Good night, Mothers; we're going to leave you now." The strains of a good night bugle faded away as the spotlight dimmed and the boys fled across the grass and over the hill to their makeshift sleeping accommodations.

Words were few now, the mothers returning to their bunks with lumps in their throats and tears in their eyes. But they were tears of joy for a once-in-a-lifetime experience.

Sunday dinner was furnished by the boys and was much enjoyed by the parents. Mothers were the special guests, with their sons doing all the work. It was a true Mother's Day.

Father's Day was celebrated in the fall of the year, and the Chaffees returned to "College Town" once again to enjoy the football game scheduled for that weekend, this time in honor of the fathers. It happened that on that particular weekend, Purdue was playing Michigan State. Roger's father had attended State for a short time and, for the sake of rivalry, rooted for the Michigan team. State won, and Don Chaffee had a good time ribbing the fraternity boys that Saturday evening.

Phi Kappa Sigma meant a great deal to Roger, and when he received his fraternity pin, he thoughtfully ordered a miniature of the skull and cross bones to present to his mother. Memento number two joined memento number one, his Eagle Scout pin.

During his junior year, Roger's studies in the aeronautics wind tunnel necessitated his commuting back and forth to the airport, a distance of eight miles or so. This called for a means of transportation in order to keep up with the airport schedule and enable him to make his campus classes, so he shopped around and found a 1954 Chevrolet for about $500. This car his parents purchased for him. In a few years the insurance cost was more than the worth of the car, but it served its purpose.

Having his own car enabled him to get home at least every two or three weeks. As in the past he usually was accompanied by a number of friends from school and always by a bundle of laundry. Twenty or twenty-five shirts to wash and iron on a weekend, plus underclothing and socks, was not unusual, and of course there was always mending. But the Chaffees looked forward to these visits and learned to care a great deal for John and Ken, Roger's very close friends. True, there were times when Father jokingly threatened to paint a sign for the front of the house reading, "Chaffee's Hotel and Laundry Service."

Ken often spoke of his arrival at Purdue. Alone and a complete stranger in West Lafayette, with less than one dollar in his pocket, he was uneasy and not a little lonely. He liked to recall how, landing at the fraternity house, he encountered Roger running out the front door to greet him as if he had known him "for at least twenty years."

Roger excelled in many of his subjects but remained outstanding in mathematics. He applied to the Dean and was given a job at the University teaching freshman math. He enjoyed this assignment very much, and it contributed to his self-confidence as well as to his finances.

At the end of that same year, Roger was again scheduled for a trip to sea for his Naval training. This trip took him aboard the destroyer *USS Perry*, cruising the North Atlantic and visiting Denmark and Sweden.

When he returned from this trip, however, he was unable to find employment for the remainder of the summer. Time hung heavily on his hands since he was never one to be idle. He read and studied a great deal but for diversion decided to build something he had never attempted before, a large model of a sailing ship.

Once more the old card table made an appearance, along with a box of material and plans for the *Cutty Sark*. He started with a roughly carved hull, a sack full of small blocks, spars, ropes, eyelets and the other necessary parts, but the summer ended too soon, and the *Cutty Sark* was not finished. The ship had to be packed away in the attic until another time when Roger would be home to work on it.

Thanksgiving weekend, Christmas holiday and spring vacation all contributed to the final completion of the *Cutty Sark*. Then it was exhibited in all its glory of full sail while Roger stood back and examined it with pride and admiration. It was a large ship and beautifully finished. "There are a lot of hours in that," he said. "Too bad to have it sit around and gather dust."

He decided that it was, in fact, too good to leave behind. He made hurried trips to the hardware store for glass and to his uncle's house where he used his electric tools, all of which made the number of vacation hours remaining even shorter. But like everything else he did, once his mind was made up to take the ship back to school with him, he let nothing stand in the way of it. Soon the case was put together, black paint applied and a small copper plaque, etched with *"The Cutty Sark"* in Roger's scrawl, attached to the frame.

The ship accompanied Roger back to Purdue where it graced the top of the bookcase in the new office he had just inherited as a result of the last election of the fraternity. The young men had honored Roger by electing him as their president — an early recognition of his leadership abilities.

From here the *Cutty Sark* traveled to Norfolk, Virginia; Pensacola, Florida; Kingsville, Texas; Jacksonville, Florida; Sanford, Florida; Fairborn, Ohio, and on to Houston, Texas. It now sails in majestic glory atop the long dresser in the bedroom of Roger's son, Stephen.

Stephen Chaffee gazes at the beautiful Cutty Sark model made by his father, Roger. Wide World Photo

5

Martha and the Flying Machines

Somehow the handsome Roger had arrived at his junior year in college with no serious romance having developed. He had dated, of course, but up until now his many activities and interests, in addition to the heavy work load he carried in studies, had consumed nearly all his time.

That year he became engrossed with two loves — one for the flying machines, the other for Martha Horn. The first was really a revival of a love that had never died. The second was excitingly new.

In September of 1955, Roger decided to investigate the possibilities among the new crop of freshman girls, and he and a fraternity friend made arrangements for a blind date. Since Roger was shorter than his friend, he agreed to take the shorter girl — her name was Martha Horn.

That evening while they played miniature golf, Roger inspected his date closely. She was a very pretty, brown haired, brown eyed girl from Oklahoma. She appeared to be very intelligent and capable, was a good listener and very feminine. His first impression, however, was that, with all her beauty and graces, she was a naive Southern girl.

Martha said later she had sized him up that first date, too, deciding that he was a handsome but smart-alec upperclassman! They seemed to be opposites in every way, and the basic law of physics held true; attracted they were. That fall they dated regularly, and by the time school was recessed for Christmas vacation, Roger had asked Martha to wear his fraternity pin. She did not give her answer right away but told him she would think it over during the holidays.

This matter was one Roger did not confide to his parents. He was not given to discussing his girl friends, and, besides, at this point he was too uncertain as to the outcome. When he broke "the news" to them, he wanted it to be an accomplished fact!

He was happy and relieved when in January, 1956, Martha accepted the pin. To celebrate they went bowling. Roger's bowling score had always been higher than Martha's, and she recalled later that she resolved to show "that smart young northerner" how to bowl! But Roger outscored her again. She consoled herself with the thought that she was just too excited to bowl well, knowing, meanwhile, she didn't really mind.

When the next school year rolled around, the romance was still in full bloom. Martha, with all her charms was unusually attractive. By her sophomore year, she had become very popular at Purdue, and it was decided that she should make a bid for the title of Homecoming Queen. Her victory was no surprise to Roger, who had already decided to make her *his* queen.

Although it was now his senior year, Roger continued to make time for the important extra curricular things — like Martha Horn. When the Chaffees visited Purdue that fall of 1956, he introduced them to Martha. Taking his father aside, he said simply, "Dad, I've gone out with a lot of girls, but this is *it*. Some day I'll marry Martha."

That early October in 1956 was an exciting time for Martha. She was about to be initiated into Kappa Alpha Theta, but this paled beside an even greater event. On October 12 Roger asked her to become his wife. The proposal came on an evening when Martha was afflicted with a severe case of laryngitis and was unable to make herself heard on the telephone to tell her parents the exciting news. Since he knew she was eager, as any girl would be, to share her joy with her parents, Roger made the call for her. In his usual straightforward manner he informed the Horns that he was about to become their son-in-law. They had, of course, met Roger by now and were very pleased with the engagement announcement.

Christmas vacation of 1956 Martha went home to Oklahoma City to begin preparations for a summer wedding. Roger went home to Grand Rapids to spend the holidays — the last Christmas with his parents as an unmarried man.

Over the years, bit by bit, items of Roger's youth had disappeared from his home. That particular Christmas Eve his scouting equipment made a last appearance from the closet. The uniform was complete with shirt, trousers, cap, merit badge sash, bedroll, flashlight, knife and utensil kit. "What's to be done with all this?" Roger asked.

"Someday," he went on, "I intend to get back into scouting, but I can't think of that now. By the time I'm ready for that, I'll certainly need a new outfit."

He stepped to the phone and called Hap, the Scoutmaster of his old Troop and an old school friend and brother Scout. After the usual friendly salutations, Roger presented his idea.

"Would you know of a boy that could use my scouting equipment, including the uniforms and sleeping bag?"

"I sure do," replied an overjoyed Hap. "We have the very boy right in our troop. He's a good Scout, too. He walks half way across town to get to Scout meetings no matter what the weather, and he hasn't missed one night all year."

"That's good enough for me," replied Roger. "Come on over and take me to him."

Roger hurried to the drug store for special wrapping paper while his folks searched the house for boxes. At the end of a busy hour three packages lay neatly wrapped and ribboned awaiting Hap's arrival. The only items Roger kept were two sashes — merit badge and Order of the Arrow.

Roger never disclosed who received the boxes. He would only say that the boy lived alone with his widowed mother, who wept for joy as she had accepted the packages. The boxes containing Roger's scouting equipment were the only gifts her son was to receive that Christmas.

The last semester of Roger's senior year was even busier than the first. He was still teaching a freshman class in mathematics and doing special tutoring on the side. Always careful not to do the work for his students, he taught them very thoroughly how to arrive at the answers for themselves. Roger detested a cheat and never knowingly catered to one.

It was necessary for Chaffee to squeeze in time for yet another project when the boys of the fraternity house voted to remodel their library. An overwhelming vote of approval got the project off to a good start, and at first there was plenty of help. As time went on, however, the carpenters and electricians fell by the wayside, one by one. Only Roger and a few of the "old faithfuls" kept at it, finally completing the job on the eve of the annual Mother's Day visit.

New bookcases, ceiling tile and paneling were installed; the floors were refinished and new light switches purchased for indirect lighting. With new drapes and matching upholstered furniture, the library was indeed a pretty sight.

It was during this last semester that Chaffee began flying at the Purdue University Airport. The story of his flight training was released March 20, 1967, in the *Purdue University News*:

> Roger Chaffee had all of the troubles that bother any new student pilot, but his instructors say it was obvious he wanted to be a good flyer.
>
> Chaffee took his first pilot training at the Purdue University Airport as a cadet in the Naval Reserve Officers Training Corps at the university. Advanced ROTC students got flight training under contract with the Purdue Aeronautics Corp., a university affiliate which operated flight training programs as a forerunner of the Aviation Technology Department.
>
> David W. Kress, now supervising inspector for the Federal Aviation Agency at South Bend, Indiana, flew with Chaffee at Purdue as an FAA examiner at Chaffee's 13-hour check as well as on his final check for graduation and approval for a private pilot license. It was Kress who recommended Chaffee for further military pilot training.
>
> "Mr. Chaffee impressed me as being good military pilot material and intent on making a career as a Navy pilot." Kress recalls. "His ability was above average, and I recall him to be very conscientious and serious about his flying career."
>
> A Cessna 172 would have to be considered pretty tame for an astronaut who, as a Navy pilot, logged 2,200 flying hours, mostly in jets. But to Chaffee in 1957 the Cessna

172 was a challenge and he had the normal problems with this easy-to-fly plane that all rookie pilots have.

He took his first Purdue ride with John R. "Pop" Stair, a real aviation old-timer, now retired. It was a 55-minute orientation flight on March 5, 1957. Two days later, he had another hour's flight time and his instructor wrote: "Landing attempts rough — tends to gain altitude." (Gaining altitude on turns is usually a case of tenseness, say flight instructors.)

Chaffee's log shows he had several instructors throughout his flight training at Purdue. These included, besides Stair, Leon W. Frost, now an instructor of army pilots at Fort Rucker, Alabama, and Charles C. Forrester and Ray

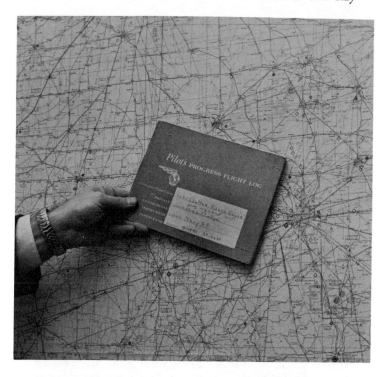

Chaffee Progress Flight Log. Purdue News Bureau Photo

Thomas, now both Lake Central Airlines captains and graduates of Purdue's professional pilot curriculum.

Chaffee flew next on March 12 and, all in all, had a good day. He worked 50 minutes on spins and stalls and the log entry noted these as "okay." Another 30 minutes were spent on slips. Said the log, "Worked some on slips — brought back to pattern — good correction for cross-winds. Progress OK."

Two days later, Chaffee flew one hour and the instructor commented, "Needs cross wind landing practice. Needs more practice on drift work — has theory. Good progress."

Things began to look brighter a week later on March 21. Though he still needed more work — especially on traffic patterns — the instructor that day said he "should be ready for solo soon."

He was. One more hour of dual instruction on March 24 brought another "good progress" report as Chaffee practiced take-offs and landings and airspeed control in glides and climbs (which "needed some work").

"Pop" Stair signed Chaffee's "ready-to-solo" certificate on March 29, and Chaffee for the first time in his life climbed behind the controls of the blue-and-white Cessna and flew a 35-minute solo flight. Afterward, Ray Thomas took him up for 25 minutes of dual time and returned to write: "Very good progress for this stage."

On April 9, Chaffee's instructor reported after one hour of dual time that there was "good progress all around."

The next day, Chaffee got in an hour of solo time and 55 minutes of dual time with Kress, who gave him his 13-hour FAA check. Wrote Kress: "13 hour check above average for (this) stage. Good coordination, judgment. Needs practice in rectangular course, S-turns. Uses excess rudder on stall recoveries. Recommend continuation."

Chaffee made his first dual cross-country flight on April 12. The three-hour trip took them to Fort Wayne, thence to Muncie and back to Lafayette. Wrote his instructor: "Worked on dead reckoning, pilotage and V.O.R. (omni range, radio navigation). Understands well enough for FAA check. Did some communication with Lafayette and Fort Wayne radio. No tower work. Landed at Fort Wayne, circled Muncie. OK for solo cross-country flight. Throttle control on take-off too abrupt."

Three days later, Chaffee was back again for more practice. After that session, the entry read: "Practiced S-turns and stall recoveries. These were maneuvers written up at 13 hour check. Altitude in low work varies about 100 to 200 feet. Otherwise competent for flight check in these maneuvers. Stall recoveries now OK. Broke out and into patterns a little high."

On May 7, Thomas took Chaffee on another dual cross-country flight, this time to Indianapolis 60 miles southeast. Chaffee performed well and was "very good in all phases."

At his 27 hour check, Kress wrote: "Tends to hold top aileron on left turns — fair execution of other maneuvers. Recommend continuation."

The next day Chaffee worked on maneuvers again. His instructor wrote: "Stalls, 1080s (three complete 360-degree turns), traffic patterns need smoothing up. Has good feel of airplane. Needs to smooth up drift correction."

Five days later, on May 22, his Purdue Aeronautics Corp. check ride resulted in this entry: "Rough on coordination. Average execution of advanced stalls, high work fair, altitude varies on low work. Rough on wind correction on pattern work. Recommended for graduation and private flight test."

Kress administered this test on May 24, afterward writing: "Final check above average — all maneuvers satisfactory. 86 per cent (grade, which is considered above average) — recommended for further military flight training."

With all this flying activity, graduation day suddenly came very near. Chaffee still had to make up the Marine training he had missed two years previously when he had used the time to attend summer school. He could not receive his Ensign's commission until this training was completed. Since there were about five or six weeks remaining between graduation and the beginning of his basic training at Norfolk, Virginia, he looked for employment opportunities and finally settled on one offered by Douglas Aircraft in Los Angeles, California.

His new employers informed him he could report for work on June 3. Commencement was not to take place until the following week so Roger requested and received special permission to be excused from commencement exercises in view of the promising job in Los Angles. On June 2, 1957, Roger received his coveted degree:

Bachelor of Science in
Aeronautical Engineering
With Distinction

It was a happy day for the Chaffee family, and to crown the occasion, Roger also received a key to the National Society of Engineers for his excellent scholastic standing during his four years of college. The key was added to his collection of Phi Kappa Sigma, Tau Beta Pi and Sigma Gamma Tau fraternity pins.

At the close of his college days Roger made this comment: "It took me four years to learn how little I knew. Knowledge is vast. There is so much more to learn, and I am going to take advantage of every opportunity that comes along."

Graduation for Roger was over, and the next day he was on the job at the Douglas Aircraft plant in California. He enjoyed the work, and it kept him busy during the daytime. Evenings were another matter. By himself in a strange city he was lonely, so he found an evening job selling cars for commission only. He did sell a few, and the profit went into his savings for the wedding which was coming in August.

It was soon time for him to leave California for the completion of his naval training. From Los Angeles to Norfolk, then down to Corpus Christi made a great deal of traveling back and forth across the United States. His Marine training was at Norfolk, and he afterward completed his work at Corpus Christi. The end of this training would bring him his commission and assignment to full Naval duty.

Wedding plans were well formulated by that time. Martha was at home in Oklahoma City, as she says, "learning to cook and do other wifely duties."

Naturally, each time Roger breezed past Oklahoma en route from one coast to the other, he stopped off to see Martha, assure her of his love and catch up on latest changes in wedding plans. Almost as an afterthought, he also brought his laundry!

Martha's father commented: "We had all sorts of good things to eat, and we sure lived high on the hog. Then all of a sudden we were in the laundry business." But realizing Michigan was a long way from Oklahoma, the Horns were happy to pinch-hit for Mom Chaffee.

On August 22, 1957, Roger completed his Naval training and received his commission as an Ensign in the United States Navy. Two days later the long-awaited wedding took place. Roger's sister Donna, her son David and Roger's parents arrived in Oklahoma City for the wedding and went to the Horn's home where they enjoyed a delicious barbecued chicken dinner in the back yard. Roger was fond of barbecues, and especially enjoyed the closeness of the hour.

The following day everyone was busy with last minute preparations for the wedding and for the rehearsal dinner which the Chaffees held for the wedding party that night. Everything went smoothly, and the dinner was a satisfying success. The whole evening was exciting and fun-filled, in spite of the fact that the temperature registered 104 degrees.

Winnie the Pooh, a tiny Pomeranian puppy which was one of their wedding gifts, became the life of the party. Pooh was destined to become a permanent member of the new Chaffee family.

As most such formal and stately occasions, this one had its lighter moments that would bring laughter in the later safety of recollection. One of the more memorable catastrophes was Roger's discovery that during his recent rigorous Marine training he had lost so much weight he was suddenly too small for the pants of his dress white uniform! With only minutes left before the ceremony, a great scramble ensued to find the necessary safety pins which would allow the bridegroom to be properly trousered.

Four years of college had required hard study and perseverance, and flight training had been difficult. Marine training was even harder, and Roger had sailed calmly through it all. But *this* — this demanded a completely different type of courage!

In the hectic bustle of the final minutes preceding the wedding march, Roger drew his father aside and, wiping his furrowed brow, remarked, "Dad, I wouldn't want to go through this again for anything in the world."

The fatherly reply was, "Well, son, if you handle things well, it will never be necessary."

Roger, in his usual efficient manner, had made motel reservations in advance and had left his car in front of this room. What he did not know was that a "friend" had taken the liberty of canceling those reservations.

When the newlyweds arrived at the motel, Roger proudly produced the key that he had called for in advance and opened the door. What a surprise to find someone else's clothing and suitcases scattered around the room! Fortunately, no one was there at the time, and the understanding proprietor made arrangements for Roger and Martha to have another room at the opposite end of the motel.

Shortly after Roger and Martha had entered their new room, a number of the wedding guests, who had been driving about town looking for them, discovered Roger's car parked in front of the room he had reserved originally. The surprised occupants of that room were rudely awakened in the wee hours of the morning by a group of noisy people serenading them with wedding songs! The bride and groom shared a satisfying last laugh as they listened to their friends serenading the wrong persons.

The next day they left on a two-week honeymoon trip to Colorado. Visits to Pike's Peak, the Cave of the Winds, Seven Falls, Cripple Creek and many of the parks in that area — brought them a new awareness of the beauty of nature. The grandeur of these sights was more moving because they were seeing them together. It was, they agreed, a truly wonderful trip.

6

Navy Man

After the honeymoon, Roger was to report aboard the *Lake Champlain* for a six-week cruise. When he arrived at Norfolk, however, his ship had already sailed, and he was then assigned to temporary duty there. Martha was able to join him in Norfolk, and they found a furnished apartment. The apartment was not everything they could have wished for, but it was their first home together, and that made it special.

Their stay in Norfolk was brief. By November, 1957, they were on the move again — this time to Pensacola, Florida, where Roger started his military flight training. Flying the T-34 first, he soon transferred to the T-28. Roger's great enthusiasm and love for flying made for rapid progress in the training program.

His advanced studies and instruction made him even more eager to move ahead, since each new advancement allowed him a different and larger plane to fly. The next summer, he was transferred to Kingsville, Texas, for more advanced training in the F9F Cougar jet fighter.

This training was very intensive, and it was during his stay in

71

Kingsville that he discovered the relaxation of working with wood. The military base had a wealth of fine tools and facilities, of which he made use in his limited leisure hours. It was an entertaining change from daily routine.

His first project was a very beautiful coffee table, a pleasant surprise to his family and friends, who had not known of Roger's fine talent for this type of craftsmanship. He had participated in the excellently executed job of installing wood paneling and bookcases at his fraternity house during his college days, but this had hardly demonstrated his apparently gifted woodworking ability. Later, in Houston, he refinished the table, and it became a prized furnishing in their home.

On November 17, 1958, in Kingsville, Texas, baby Sheryl joined the Chaffee household. Her arrival was timely for Roger was scheduled to leave the very next day for his first carrier training. He disliked leaving his family at this time but was thankful to have been with Martha when their baby daughter was born.

The weeks and months passed quickly, and early in 1959 Roger completed his Navy flight training. Martha very proudly pinned his wings in place at graduation. As had been his habit on previous occasions Roger purchased a duplicate set of miniature wings for his mother. She now had three cherished symbols of the steppingstones in the life of her son.

In March, 1959, Roger and Martha started on their way to bigger things at Jacksonville, Florida. They detoured on this trip to allow themselves time to stop off in Oklahoma City for a visit with Martha's parents; then they went on to Michigan to spend a little time with Roger's family. Their "long way 'round" from Texas to Florida was a family joke for some time to come.

This was the Chaffees' first look at their new little granddaughter, and they were overjoyed to have a baby girl in their home again, even for a short time. Grandfather Don, holding Sheryl gently against his shoulder, once rocked himself as well as the baby to sleep. On seeing this, Roger remarked, "It was worth all that long drive up here just to see Dad and Sheryl together like this."

Furnished-apartment living had become "old hat" to Roger and Martha, and consequently they had begun, piece-by-piece, to accumulate some furnishings of their own. These had been packed and shipped on their way to Jacksonville so as to be waiting for them on their arrival.

In the meantime, Roger knew that his 1957 Plymouth station wagon and motel rooms would be "home" for his wife and daughter from the time they left Michigan until they could find a house in Jacksonville. Houses there were at a premium that spring, but they were fortunate to find a pretty little cottage on Peter Pan Place within two days after their arrival. They bought the house and were able to take immediate possession.

The younger Chaffees set up housekeeping with all the fun and enthusiasm that most young couples enjoy in settling the first new home of their own. King Roger and Queen Martha — their kingdom, their home.

Even with the small Sheryl to attend to, it was not long before the last box was emptied and their home for three was settled.

Chaffee's first assignment at Jacksonville was in overhaul and repair of the A3D twin-engined jet photo reconnaissance plane. The A3D was an advanced airplane and for this reason had been flown only by older pilots with the rank of Lieutenant Commander or above. Roger, however, became so familiar with the plane that he was allowed to pilot one, becoming one of the youngest pilots ever to fly the A3D.

During the summer of 1959 the Chaffees were able to visit Roger and his family at Jacksonville. The folks had gathered together all of Roger's possessions left at home and packed them into the car for the trip to Florida. This included such items as his electric train, the small rocking chair that had been his birthday gift at the age of two, the Indian headdress he had made at Scout camp, sports numerals and letters earned in high school and his great grandfather's cavalry sword from the Civil War, a gift from his grandfather. As Roger knew, it was difficult for his parents to part with all these mementos. It was the end of an era for the elder Chaffees.

Too soon, it was time to say good-bye. Parting was always difficult. This time Mike's tears were very much in evidence, and though Don tried to hide his tears, he was not completely successful. Roger and Martha tried to console them with hugs and the reassurance that they soon would be together again.

Partings had always been hard for this affectionate family.

Even when Roger had been at Purdue and they had seen him fairly often, those goodbyes had always been the same.

The career conscious military man must always be prepared to move on. February, 1960, Roger again moved his family — this time to Sanford, Florida. He was moving on, not only, but up, as well, thoroughly enjoying his rapid advancement. Their house would have to be sold. In the meantime, unable to find a house to rent in Sanford, it was again necessary for him to buy one. Fortunately, this time the real estate company guaranteed to take it back at the end of his training period at Sanford. He was also successful in finding a buyer for his house in Jacksonville so the transition was accomplished smoothly. Roger's only objection to the new home was that there was no place for barbecues and the gatherings of friends which he so enjoyed. To meet this need he set to work and built a fine patio.

Roger's stay at Sanford lasted only about six months. He was now ready for assignment to the fleet, having previously completed his jet training at Kingsville, Texas. Every day, every week, every month brought new experiences. Time also brought an awakened awareness of the proximity of death. It was at Sanford that Roger lost one of his very close friends in a flying mishap. This incident served to strengthen all the flyers, who found it necessary to accept anew the fact that their chosen life was one requiring strong determination and a realization that life moves on in spite of such accidents and losses. After a few similar experiences, Roger coined a phrase:

"There's only room for one mistake. You can buy the farm only once."

His family accepted his way of thinking, and made it their strength too, knowing that he was happy in his way of life and in the goal he was pursuing. He knew his job, and his enthusiasm for flying was heartwarming. To climb to the top of the ladder and to be the very best he could be was his ambition in life.

After completion of his training at Sanford he was ready for assignment to active routine duties. The assignment came through, and he was happy to learn that the Navy had requested his return to Jacksonville.

The distance to move was not great this time, and everything seemed easy compared with previous migrations of the family.

They even had time to look leisurely for a new house, but it seemed the more time they had, the more particular and exacting they became. House after house was scrutinized, and their final decision took them back to Peter Pan Place, to the same street, and only a few houses away from their former home.

"Hey! Look at that, would you! They haven't even taken our name off the box!"

As they were moving into their new home, they noticed that Roger's name was still on the mailbox in front of the original home. After he had painted his name on the box in front of their new house, friends began to question him teasingly about his real estate ventures!

The return to Jacksonville found Roger assigned to V.A.P. 62, a heavy photography squadron. Along with his flying duties, he also had the responsibility of safety and quality control officer. It was in this position that his desire for perfection and order became so evident. Chaffee compiled and wrote a quality control manual that contained the applicable specifications and proper sequence of operations necessary to maintain a flight squadron of this nature. He was proud of this achievement, but some of the men working with Chaffee thought him too demanding and exacting in his expectation of perfection. They respected his judgment, however, and knew that he had their welfare at heart. One of the men said, "He's tough and an 'eager beaver,' but he doesn't ask you to do anything he wouldn't do himself — and we sure love him."

It is one of life's strange coincidences that Roger, while in V.A.P. 62, was assigned to fly over the coast of Florida and make aerial photographs of Cape Canaveral. These were used to map out the area which later was to become the launching center of the United States space program at Cape Kennedy and the Kennedy Space Center.

South of Florida, events in Cuba were the cause of new concern to the U.S. Government, which already had its hands full with problems in Berlin. The new Cuban government was so distressing to some of its citizens that by April, 1961, there were about 40,000 Cuban refugees living in Miami. It was during this time of increasing concern that Chaffee was assigned to making routine flights to Cuba, enabling him to log many flying hours. At times he made as many as three flights per day, and compiled one hundred flight hours each month. On these "shuttle" trips back and forth to Guantanamo Bay, each trip carried three men per plane, the pilot, the co-pilot and the photographer.

Sometimes they would stay on the American base at Guantanamo Bay for a day or so, and when he had leisure time, Roger would spend it fishing. On one occasion, it was necessary for the co-pilot to stay on longer to complete his assignment, and this left a few hours of wait-over for Roger. He therefore bought a twenty-five-cent mullet for bait, took a hook and roll of fishline and rowed out into the Bay. He later said he imagined himself back in Michigan. Tossing the bait over the edge of the boat he tied the other end of the line to his finger and lay down in the bottom of the boat to sun-bathe. In this way he knew he could quickly detect a bite or strike.

Suddenly a large barracuda hit his bait nearly taking his finger off! It took Chaffee about two hours to bring in the huge fish. Taking his prize back to the base, he froze it solid, packed it in dry ice and flew at a high altitude all the way back to Jacksonville. There he presented it to Martha, who was sure he had brought her some nice china from Cuba, and she admits to surprise but not disappointment on finding Roger's prize catch.

During this same tour of duty in Jacksonville, Roger took on an extra job of teaching a group of young men to fly. These were civilians who had purchased a used Taylorcraft and allowed Roger to fly it any time he wished, in exchange for flying instructions to the group.

It so happened that the Don Chaffees were visiting their son in Jacksonville at this time, so Don was happy to avail himself of the opportunity to get in some flying again.

At Jacksonville, Roger was required to put in a certain amount of time each year qualifying for flattop or carrier flight training. He spent some time aboard the USS Saratoga in both day and night flight practice. Roger's comment regarding the day flying was, "Setting that big bird down on the flight deck was like landing on a postage stamp." Night flying was considerably different. Another time he said, "Getting catapulted off that flight deck at night is like getting shot into a bottle of ink!"

Many duties and interests in Jacksonville did not prevent him from pursuing his education. Diligently studying for his Master's degree in Aeronautics, he was constantly searching for ways to advance his career. He tried, however, never to work at the expense of the welfare of others, having an ingrained and profound respect for the Golden Rule: "Do unto others as you would have them do unto you."

The Navy recognized Roger's unique capabilities and had marked him as a man with a bright future. With this on record, advanced training was arranged for him whenever feasible. On one such occasion he was sent to Africa on a cruise, and it was during this tour of duty on July 3, 1961, that Stephen was born in Oklahoma City, Oklahoma. When Roger came back from Africa, he first viewed his new son. The family was now complete — Roger, Martha, Sheryl and Stephen. He was able to spend some time with the family, but a short time later was sent to Safety and Reliability School in California.

Roger was usually so efficient and sure of himself that it was refreshing for his friends to learn of an experience that revealed him just as human as the rest of them.

At Jacksonville Roger and Martha had an eighteen-foot boat with a fifty-horsepower engine. In his astute manner Roger observed that it would be a simple matter for someone to hook onto his boat trailer some night and roll away with the whole works. In order to prevent this, he threaded a chain through the motor, boat and trailer and then ran it through the utility room door and around a large pail. It was an amazingly efficient method, and Roger confidently observed that if anyone was going to steal his boat, they would have to take half his house, as well!

A few weeks later Roger, at home for a Saturday, was eager to get the boat into the water. Telling Martha that he was going on ahead and that she and the children should come along later in the other car, he bounded out of the house, hitched the boat to his high powered station wagon and took off!

Surveying the resultant wreckage of the utility room door, he informed Martha that she really should have told him that he was still "anchored." He didn't mind that the joke was on him, and he was the first to relate the mishap to their friends. He always could enjoy a laugh on himself. It was certain that he did become angry about little things sometimes, but on this occasion, at least, he enjoyed the joke.

After the younger Chaffees were resettled in Jacksonville,

Roger's parents made a trip to see their new grandson. Their visit was cut short in order to avoid an approaching hurricane. They waited almost too long. On the morning of their departure Roger followed them down to the fork in the road where they turned north for Michigan, and he turned south toward the base where he, as the duty officer, was responsible for the security of the planes. The storm was a fairly bad one.

Martha was marooned for a time by high water which made travel by car impossible. Not wanting to be alone with the children, she took refuge with neighbors during the height of the storm. A few houses and carports were shifted on their foundations, but there was no severe damage. Roger, unable to get back home, spent the time on the Naval base.

The unstable weather, accepted and endured by residents, seemed to Martha in marked contrast to the dependable Roger, admired for the stability of his own character and ambitions.

7

"Dad, I'm In!"

On February 20, 1962, Roger arrived in Grand Rapids for a
two-weeks' visit, sandwiched between assignments. It happened
to be at the time of John Glenn's Freedom 7 flight, and the
family gathered around the television with what was thought
to be equal enthusiasm.

Did Chaffee have plans for a part in the space program even
at that early date? If so, his reserved nature allowed him to
make no mention of it, but shortly after the Freedom 7 shot
it was learned that a new group of astronauts was being sought.
When his parents visited Roger in August, he confided to his
father that he had made application for the astronaut training
program. Later, Roger admitted he had indicated to his supe-
riors that he wanted to train as test pilot for astronaut status.

Homeward bound, Don made the decision to tell Mike. Roger
had wanted to spare his mother unnecessary concern in case he
was not accepted, but his father decided that she was capable
of accepting and sharing Roger's ambition with understanding,
if not with joy. Both agreed it was his life to live and give.

That fall, October, 1962, was the beginning of the qualifying tests which Roger took along with the 1800 other applicants throughout the United States.

October was a turbulent month that year. For it was just after Roger started his qualifying tests that the Cuban crisis arose. It had been discovered, from photographs obtained in aerial flights over Cuba, that Russian planes and missle installations were mushrooming in that country, only 90 miles from the tip of the Florida mainland. The Americans had learned that at the push of a button missles could be lobbed to many American cities. Meetings in the White House were conducted for a week prior to any national announcement and with such secrecy that no word had leaked.

So it was that the visiting Russian diplomat, Gromyko, departed on Saturday, bound for his homeland, with no apparent inkling that the U.S. had discovered their secret.

On Monday noon, October 22nd, Press Secretary Pierre Salinger told more than 400 reporters that the President would speak to the nation that night on a "matter of the highest national urgency." United States military units around the world were alerted.

Then President John F. Kennedy informed the nation of his decision to "quarantine" Cuba — in a naval blockade — with the American ships carrying orders to intercept and sink, if necessary, any Russian ship proceeding to Cuba with military supplies.

This action placed the United States at the brink of World War III, and those were anxious days. For several days during that tense time, the fate of the world hung in the balance. Then the Russians acceded, (their ships had already veered off course), and Secretary of State Dean Rusk made his famous "eyeball" statement. "We're eyeball to eyeball," he remarked to someone, "and the other fellow just blinked."

It was a turning point in U.S.-Russian relations.

The time had now come for Roger to reconsider his Naval career. He had logged over 1800 hours of flying time, and his tour of sea duty was over. The Navy offered him the opportunity to work further on his Master's degree. Eager to take advantage of this offer, he prepared to move the family to the Air Force Institute of Technology at Wright-Patterson Air Force

Base, Dayton, Ohio. The term was to start March 4, 1963, and it was time to say goodbye to their many friends in Jacksonville.

Both Roger and Martha loved people and parties, and with their anticipated departure as an excuse, they decided to host a New Year's Eve party for Roger's entire squadron. The men and their wives, numbering nearly 100, milled through the house with much laughter and gaiety. The food was excellent, the comradeship even better. It was a gathering long recalled with nostalgia, even though for Martha, it had its somewhat less than joyous moments. One such was the squadron's presentation of a dress sword to Roger. Naval tradition required that an officer receiving a new sword allow the old one to be broken. Since Roger's original sword had been a very beautiful, artistically engraved gift from Martha, she had deliberated at length about allowing them to make the gift. But her pride in the knowledge that her husband's comrades loved and respected him enough to want to do this for him overrode her hesitation. Later the broken pieces of sword were crossed, mounted on a red velvet background and encased in a glass covered frame that was to hang in the den of their Houston home along with the beaver-tail-shaped paddle marked "Eager Beaver," also given him by squadron V.A.P. 62.

The wee hours of that New Year's morning found Roger and Martha clearing away the remains of a successful party and putting their home in order. They were expecting prospective buyers at 10:00 a.m., and everything had to be in apple pie order for Martha, shipshape for Roger.

Happily, the house was sold without delay. Now it was time to leave for Michigan. Clothing for Michigan's January weather and some of the family's choicest possessions were packed into the station wagon and Martha's little Sunbeam. A sturdy towbar was made for the Sunbeam and attached to the wagon, and the Sunbeam rolled along behind as the family of four headed merrily for Grand Rapids.

On January 19, 1963, about 5:00 p.m., Roger called his parents to tell them that he and the family were just north of Indianapolis, Indiana, and had decided to come all the way in spite of the bad weather.

At 11:45 p.m, the waiting parents noticed two cars stalled on the icy incline of their street. They watched for a few moments from their living room window, and deciding help was needed, Don Chaffee grabbed his coat and boots and went to the assistance of the occupants. He was happy indeed that he had decided to play the "good Samaritan" when he discovered that it was Roger and his family, stalled less than a hundred and fifty feet from home!

It was a weary family that scrambled for the warm food and beds waiting for them. Don and Mike Chaffee, when they finally retired, did so with the happy knowledge that the children were safe at home once more, at least for a time.

The younger Chaffees spent three enjoyable weeks with Roger's parents. Many of their evenings were spent enjoying rousing games of contract bridge; and although Stephen was still too small to participate in the out-of-door games, Sheryl was boldly introduced to the abundant piles of snow, in which she and her daddy romped happily building snowmen and throwing snowballs. The snow was a new experience for the Southern-born little girl.

As March 4 neared, and the beginning of his new assignment, Roger went on to Dayton, leaving Martha and the children with his parents in Grand Rapids. It was time for him to sign in at Wright-Patterson Air Force Base and to find a home for his family.

With his usual thoroughness, he set about immediately making the necessary arrangements that would allow the family to join him. Within a few days his call came to the waiting Martha. He had found a house in Fairborn, Ohio, a suburb near Dayton. He was especially pleased because the owner had agreed to rent the house. To Roger, who already had had his name on three mortgages, this was appreciated particularly.

That weekend Don and Mike Chaffee drove Martha and the children to Fairborn. As they got out of the car and climbed the steps, they were greeted by a happy Roger, waiting at the open door to welcome his wife and children to their already partially settled new home.

The household goods had arrived in Fairborn some time ahead of Roger, so he had had a few days before Martha's arrival in which to unpack many of the boxes. He had, in fact, worked hard to make this rented house appear home-like, and had stocked the cupboards and refrigerator with groceries. He even had prepared a meal for the hungry travelers, remembering to cook some of the family's favorite dishes.

Over the next several months, Roger and Martha were able to spend more time with his parents than had been possible since his marriage. Fairborn was close enough to Grand Rapids to make weekend visits feasible, the families exchanging visits both ways.

By June 18, 1963, the number of astronaut candidates had been reduced to 271, and examinations became increasingly competitive. Chaffee was tested, screened and investigated over and over again. One physical test revealed that he had a very small lung capacity, but that he used what he had to better advantage than most people with a large lung capacity.

When the tests were completed, he commented to Martha, "They managed to thoroughly humiliate us at least three times a day!"

In early October of that year, Roger had a few free days between terms, and he and a friend, Burt (Bill) Miller, decided it would be a good time to go deer hunting in Michigan. It was an anxious time for Chaffee with the names of the third group of astronauts to be released sometime within the next two weeks. Tension was mounting by the day, and it was agreed by all that the bow and arrow hunting would be a refreshing change during this difficult time of waiting.

They secured their hunting licenses, packed the gear in the station wagon, assembled some necessary food in the portable cooler and headed for the north woods.

Michigan was movingly beautiful with the trees flaunting their leaves of brilliant golds, reds, oranges and browns. It was Chaffee's first visit to Michigan's wooded areas since scouting days, and both he and Bill very much enjoyed the opportunity for camping in the unseasonably balmy October weather. On the return trip they informed their families that though they had seen a few deer, they had not shot at any. They considered the trip by no means a failure, however, since it had afforded some much needed rest and relaxation.

The two hunters returned to Fairborn on October 14, 1963, and found a message there asking Roger to call the NASA Headquarters in Houston, Texas. This was it! He couldn't reach the phone fast enough! Gripping the telephone tightly, he heard the coveted words. He had been selected as one of fourteen new astronauts to be named to the United States space program. He and Martha were elated over the news but were under strict orders to inform no one until the official announcement was made later that week.

On Friday, October 18, Roger flew to Houston and there was formally introduced to the news media as one of the new astronauts. The news was out. He immediately telephoned his parents in Grand Rapids. His first words were, "Dad, I'm in!"

"That's wonderful, son. Congratulations," came the reply. He had reached for and achieved another high goal, and he felt their rejoicing with him and their great pride in his success.

In Grand Rapids a press conference was called at the Chaffee's home. His parents learned quickly that as parents of an astronaut they would enter a completely foreign way of life. They were news too. With excitement and happiness they discussed their reactions with the reporters.

"Roger's voice on the phone telling of his appointment was most exhilarating. We just had to be happy for him. We knew he'd make it. There wasn't a minute of doubt in our minds. Roger always wanted to be the best. There was only one way for him, the perfect way; nothing less would do." This from Don.

"Naturally," he continued, "his mother and I will worry a bit. But our hearts are content, knowing that our son is doing exactly what he wants to do."

In answer to a question concerning Roger's childhood, Mr. Chaffee replied, "We built model airplanes together. You could describe our father-son relationship as an ideal one. We were very close and still are. Perhaps you would say he was an all-American boy."

The thoughtful reaction of Roger's mother to his appointment was, "That's what he's lived for, dreamed of and worked for, so I'm glad that's what he can do. Roger was not a bookworm, by any means. He was just an all-around boy, with the normal American boy's interests in the things that make the sum total of life. But he was the kind of boy who could make up his mind as to what he wanted to do and what he wanted to be and set himself with determination to achieve his objectives.

"Martha deserves tremendous credit. His accomplishment requires a lot of studying, which can be demanding on family life. This is what he wanted so we share his happiness with him. What more can parents ask than that their son shall have achieved another steppingstone toward a further objective. Roger is happy to give himself to the world in this, his chosen way."

In Fairborn, Martha had a most difficult time trying to keep the secret of Roger's appointment. She, of course, had known the news since the hour that Roger had received the call, but in all her meetings with her friends and the other officers' wives, it was necessary to act as though this unbelievable upheaval of their lives had not occurred at all.

"I thought they'd never make the announcement," she said that Friday. "It's the hardest secret I ever kept!"

It was a busy but happy time. As soon as the news was released, their friends gathered joyously around, and there was, of course, the inevitable news conference. In a flurry of excitement, Martha told of her part in Roger's career.

"We were married when Roger went to flying school, and it's as if I've gone through every program with him. We started with the T-34, and now it's to be rockets. What's familiar doesn't frighten you, but it's only natural to be afraid of the unknown.

"We never debated Roger's going into the program. As soon as he was informed that he was eligible, he applied. That was last June. We thought we would hear about the first of October, and the waiting and suspense has been awful.

"Monday, a call came from Houston before Roger got home from Michigan, and I thought, 'Well, this is it. We'll know now one way or the other.' They didn't tell me anything, naturally, but that was the worst time of all, waiting for him to get here and call them back.

"I've been on the phone all day. We've been sitting around talking about how thrilling it all will be. Roger will be home Saturday afternoon, and I can't wait; I'm just so proud of him.

"Roger is a perfectionist in his work; whenever he sets out to do something, he gets it done."

The little Chaffees had different reactions. Four-year-old Sheryl exclaimed, "Daddy's going to be a rocket man!" Two-year-old Stephen said only, "Cookie, Mommy."

Roger called Martha's parents and informed them of the news.

"We just found out at noon," said Mr. and Mrs. Horn at a news conference. "Roger always was crazy about flying. He'd rather fly than eat.

"He's wanted to go to the moon since he was five years old. We surely hope he gets his chance. The dangers involved make us think deeply, but it also makes us extremely proud. Martha is all for it because it's what he wants. That's what any good wife wants."

Roger's own reaction to the appointment was calm confidence. In response to the questions of the reporters, he remarked, "I was very pleased with the appointment. I've wanted to fly and perform adventurous flying tasks all my life. Ever since the first seven Mercury astronauts were named, I've been keeping my studies up."

Roger returned home from Houston the following weekend, next making a quick trip to Grand Rapids to share his delight with his parents. They had every reason to be proud of him and his achievements, and they were. His appointment was proof that a boy from a family of moderate circumstances could attain high goals in his chosen field. His own wealth — a sturdy body, a strong and well-educated mind, and an everlasting drive — had put him on this plateau as one of the fourteen outstanding military men in the United States. The appointment alone is a jewel in the crown of an astronaut.

The week following the announcement, with the initial excitement over, Roger was interviewed again. In his offhand way, he said, "It was pretty lively there for a while. It seemed that almost everyone in the world called or sent wires. Even my old football coach at Central High School in Grand Rapids, Romulus Romani, got in touch. About all he said was that I sure looked different skinny. I was just about the fattest guard he had ever seen!

"Ever since I was a little shaver, my dad and I built model airplanes and flew them all year 'round. We used to put skis on them in the winter. My dad was a licensed pilot and barnstormed all over the Midwest in a Waco biplane. He's quite a guy."

A few weeks later Roger was interviewed again. At that time he said, "When I was a boy, I knew some day men would be going into space, and I wanted to go. I've made the goal

I aimed for, but now I want to be the first one on the moon, if I can.

"I'm real excited. It won't be just a throttle-jockey job; anyone can fly a plane, you know. It will be an engineering job, a tremendous scientific challenge.

"At the end of each year, the Navy asks its officers what type of duty they would aspire to. Each year I indicated I wanted to train as a test pilot for astronaut status.

"The invitation came as a surprise last June. We'd been away and came home to find a letter waiting, asking that I answer by June 18. It was the 18th the day we arrived home — I telephoned."

In response to questions about his physical tests to become an astronaut, Roger replied, "They tested my heart while I was still, while I was exercising, with a hand in icy water and while I walked up a treadmill that got progressively steeper. Three-quarters of one day they spent running electrocardiograms of my heart. I'll bet they ran off two thousand feet of paper! I'm in perfect health."

He said of Martha, "She's always been interested in the kind of work I do, and she's tremendously excited over this new assignment."

Concluding his remarks Roger answered a question concerning fear of the astronaut program. "I guess when a fellow climbs into a spacecraft, straps himself in and starts waiting for the countdown, he could give what's coming some really serious consideration, but I'm not afraid. I feel a capable pilot should be able to meet the emergencies that may develop. What's more, there's risk to flying an ordinary plane, just as there is to driving a car, walking across a street or going down a stairway.

"There's an exact, precise job here. When we reach the moon, studies done there will tell us a great deal about the solar system, and the over-all NASA program will produce great benefits for our nation and the world. It already has, in fact.

"What's more, I'll be doing something for my country, something in which I can take great pride."

The United Press news release from Houston on October 19, 1963, was strangely prophetic. It said, "America's fourteen new astronauts dream of walking in the pock-marked craters and through the dusty 'seas' of the moon. Some will make it, others may fail along the way.

"But all asked for, and have been granted, the chance — and for that alone, time and circumstances will exact a price. A steep price, for the title of astronaut does not come cheap.

"In the months ahead, these men will ride at dizzying speeds on centrifuges and feel navels reaching for backbones. They will be dumped in oceans and flown on stomach-churning dives in airplanes.

"The tortures the experts call training may seem more satanic than scientific. There will be hours in chambers hotter than the hottest day in the Sahara, and colder than the worst Antarctic can offer. And there is the altitude chamber, where all they do is remove the air.

"For these astronauts will range far afield, to industrial plants on the west coast, the firing range at White Sands, New Mexico, booster rocket facilities in New Orleans and Huntsville, Alabama, the launching pads of Cape Canaveral, 'visits of state' to Washington and weeks of living in hotels and restaurants and out of suitcases.

"In the end, doubtless, there will be frustration and failure for some. The new astronauts are confident, or they would never have been accepted. They have age, an average of 31 years, on their side. They are brilliantly educated — an average of 5.6 years of college, with two research scientists among them.

"They have the dreams, and the federal space agency says they have the brains and ability. The only barrier between them and the moon now seems to be five years at hard scientific labor."

No man knew that there was to be the final barrier of death for some.

Apollo prime crew, L-R, Virgil Grissom, Edward White II and Roger Chaffee. NASA PHOTOGRAPH

89

Water egress training in swimming pool, Ellington Air Force Base, Houston. Left, boilerplate model of spacecraft. NASA PHOTOGRAPH

Roger Chaffee prepares to enter Apollo spacecraft mock-up to begin simulated run. NASA PHOTOGRAPH

91

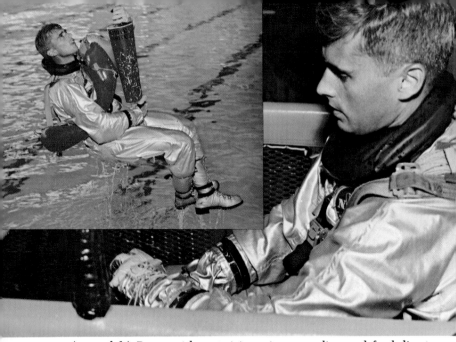

(upper left) Rescue pick-up training using same sling used for helicopter rescue. NASA PHOTOGRAPH

92 (upper right) Roger Chaffee in X15 simulator control used in pre-spaceflight training. NASA PHOTOGRAPH

(bottom) Apollo crew relaxes during their water egress training, Gulf of Mexico. NASA PHOTOGRAPH

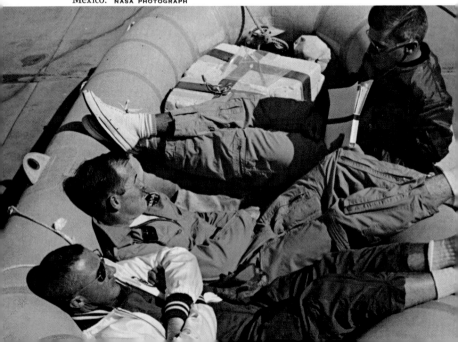

(upper) Chaffee family in their Houston home. L-R, Sheryl, Martha, Roger, Stephen. Gun cabinet shown at left. NASA PHOTOGRAPH

(lower) Third group of fourteen astronauts. Roger Chaffee is at extreme right, front row. NASA PHOTOGRAPH

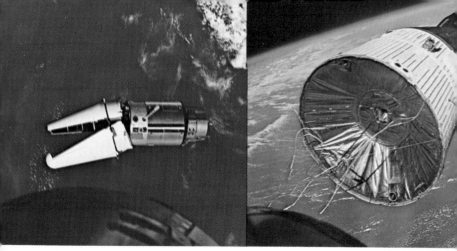

(upper left) Side view, nose of Gemini IX. Some astronauts dubbed Gemini IX, "The Angry Alligator." NASA PHOTOGRAPH

94

(upper right) Rondezvous G. T. VII 37. Docking of manned and unmanned spacecrafts. NASA PHOTOGRAPH

(bottom) Astronaut Edward White II makes walk in space from Gemini Titan IV. NASA PHOTOGRAPH

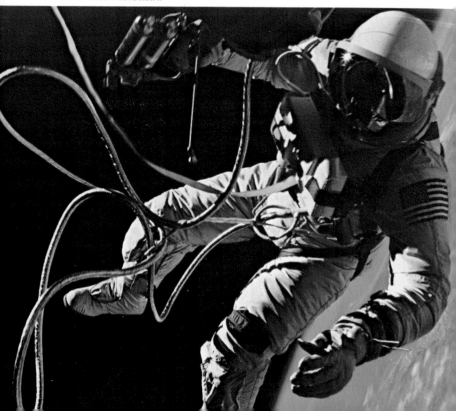

Apollo crew in space suits, during pre-flight practice at Cape Kennedy. Suit-up men behind crew, in white uniforms. NASA PHOTOGRAPH

During water egress training, Gulf of Mexico, crew talks with personnel on board NASA motor vessel, *Retriever,* October, NASA PHOTOGRAPH

8

. . . On Course

Little more than a month after Chaffee's appointment to the astronaut training program, the country was plunged suddenly within an hour into undreamed-of tragedy. Of course, *someone* had dreamed of it. The deed was finished, and on November 22, 1963, at 1:10 p.m., Kenneth O'Donnell, John F. Kennedy's assistant, painfully informed Lyndon B. Johnson, "The President is dead, Mr. President."

The people who mourned John F. Kennedy stood in various stages of shock and grief; many wept openly at the news. Even those of different political persuasion deeply regretted the tragedy. When the alleged assassin was murdered suddenly a few days later, renewed feelings of uncertainty and fear swept the country.

The events were especially close to the Roger Chaffees. There are many questions that arise at such a time, there is always some confusion. But always, in the military, there is discipline. Roger Chaffee had spent his young lifetime disciplining himself. What he had not accomplished, the Navy had.

The duties of an astronaut are numerous and varied. One of

Roger's first duties during this difficult time was a speaking engagement at Junior Achievement's first Michigan Sectional Achievers' Conference held November 29, 1963, in Grand Rapids. He showed a NASA film on space and then gave a talk, followed by a question period. He told the 500 young people in attendance, "You must move full steam ahead on any job you do; you must be the best guy in the job.

"Just think how disastrous it would be if the United States did not have the understanding and engineering knowledge to war in space should an aggressor nation decide to use space as the battle ground. We must explore space *now* and be prepared."

Roger, Martha and the children spent that somewhat subdued 1963 Thanksgiving with his parents. He and his dad took one day together and visited the Lear-Siegler Aerospace Development Center where Roger had worked one summer while attending Purdue. Then the family returned to Fairborn.

Mid-December again brought moving day. Roger terminated his stay at Wright-Patterson and sent the household goods on to Houston. He and the family then returned to Grand Rapids for a ten-day visit.

Life was changing. As a public figure, Roger now found himself singled out for various honors and opportunities for service. While visiting in Grand Rapids before going south, Roger received an invitation to speak at an all-school assembly at his alma mater Central High. Following this talk he was greatly surprised to see his old friend and fraternity brother from Purdue days, Ken Thomas, step from behind the curtain. It was an even greater surprise when Ken presented him with a fine desk, the top of which was made of beautifully colored mosaic depicting the planets in the solar system. This unique gift was greatly treasured by Roger and still stands prominently in the den of his Houston home.

They left Grand Rapids a few days before Christmas, traveling to Oklahoma City to spend the remainder of the holidays with Martha's parents.

Arrangements for housing in Houston were made by phone. When their household goods arrived they were able to move into a duplex apartment located in Clear Lake City, a suburb close to the Manned Spacecraft Center.

In February of 1964 Roger received word that the Grand

Valley Council of the Boy Scouts of America had named the Eagle Scout graduating class of 1963 in his honor. He was asked to speak at the meeting, but because astronaut training had begun in January, he was unable to attend. He arranged for his father and mother to represent him, however, and they played a tape recording of Roger's voice. Then, to the delight of the new Eagle Scouts, the Chaffees presented each one with a portrait of Roger.

Roger and his family lived in the duplex apartment for about six months. During the Christmas holidays of 1963, he completed the house plans for their new home, and they had only to choose the property on which to build. They finally discovered a beautiful lot that pleased them both, and by the middle of March their home was under construction. They hoped to be able to stay in it for some time!

By the spring of 1964 Roger's astronaut training was in full swing, and in April the fourteen new astronauts took the first of many field trips in their training program. The first one was to the Grand Canyon where two United States Geological Survey instructors guided them through the canyon, explaining the types of rocks that would be valuable to bring back from the moon. One of the projects of the first lunar landing will be to bring back 80 pounds of the lunar surface, and it was necessary to learn of what that 80 pounds should consist.

In early May, the astronauts visited the world's largest solar telescope at Kitt Peak Observatory near Tuscon, Arizona. Upon seeing the moon at such close range, Roger exclaimed, "Boy, this is something! It's the best I have ever seen. My wife and I quiz each other about places on the moon. It doesn't sound like much, but it sure beats television." Roger was not a spectator; he was a participant!

On June 6, 1964, Roger flew into Grand Rapids in his T-33 trainer jet and officially dedicated the new Kent County Municipal Airport. It was fitting that the city's own astronaut, glowing with enthusiasm and love for his work, should dedicate this new access to his hometown.

While in Grand Rapids Roger made another speech which revealed his dedication to and pride in being a part of his nation's space program. The occasion was the chartering of the new Optimist Club of West Grand Rapids. With a natural ease and confidence, Roger outlined the program of the National Aeronautics and Space Administration.

". . . I would like to talk to you about a program, a program to which I belong as an astronaut, and to which you belong as an American. It is a historic program which can be compared favorably with the exploration of the New World by Columbus or the Portuguese voyages around Africa. It is a program which will in our time reap us tremendous economic benefits and open up to our youth educational vistas of challenge to stagger the imagination. I am referring to our country's space program.

"Let's approach the topic of manned space flight as we see it today.

"First, we find ourselves having reached the closing phase of America's initial venture into the manned space field with the conclusion of the Mercury flights.

"I believe that one must agree that the things we have learned from our space effort more than justify the expenditure. One cannot help but be aware of the fact that in a little more than four years an organization has been formed which, from an austere beginning, has developed the capability of putting a man into space, keeping him there for 34 hours and 20 minutes, traversing over a half million miles at speeds of over 17,000 miles an hour, then bringing him down within 7,000 yards of a pinpointed aircraft carrier in the Pacific Ocean. I believe that when one considers this feat, the question of whether or not we are ahead of the Russians is irrelevant. As serious as the question of being ahead is, one cannot subtract from the fact that the Mercury program has been another example of the technical capability of the American people.

"From Mercury we are moving into project Gemini and Apollo. Gemini will provide us with the capability of putting two astronauts into orbit for up to two weeks. During this period we will perfect the rendezvous technique, that of bringing two vehicles together in space. The developing of this technique is all important to the Apollo program — the successor to Gemini that will land men on the moon.

"In the Gemini effort a spacecraft similar to the Mercury spacecraft will be used; however, it will have 50 per cent more capacity than the Mercury spacecraft and will weigh approximately twice as much. The rendezvous mission will be the most important single task the pilot will make during the early Gemini program. In complexity it is comparable to the mid-air refueling by high-performance aircraft, but it presents unique problems not present when operating in the atmosphere. Briefly, rendezvous involves the launching of a target vehicle — in this case an Agena engine boosted by an Atlas rocket — into an 150-mile circular earth orbit, then the launching of a Gemini spacecraft atop a Titan II within 24 hours. The pilot of the Gemini spacecraft will determine the exact moment to fire his thrusters and to align his orbital path with that of the Agena target, apply thrust until he overtakes the Agena, then thread the nose of his spacecraft into the docking collar of the Agena.

"We may then experiment with man's capability to leave his spacecraft and maneuver around the outside of his craft. Finally, we will return the Gemini spacecraft to earth in a manner similar to that of the Mercury spacecraft, at first using a parachute descent to earth. Eventually it is planned to use a device known as the paraglider, which will enable the vehicle to glide to earth like a kite and make a landing at a selected site like an airplane.

"From Gemini we will move into the Apollo program — the lunar landing effort. The Apollo spacecraft will carry three American astronauts into orbit around the moon. Then a two-man vehicle called the Lunar Excursion Module or LEM will carry two of the astronauts to the moon's surface and back in a manner similar to the use of a small boat for carrying passengers back and forth between an island and a larger craft circling some distance off shore.

"Three units, or modules, will make up the Apollo spacecraft. The unit that will house all three astronauts during transit from the earth to lunar orbit and back to earth is called the Command Module. Attached to the Command Module will be the second segment, providing rocket propulsion into and out of lunar orbit, called the Service Module. This module also carries a large electrical and oxygen supply. This module will remain with the Command Module through the mission to the moon until just before the return to the earth's atmosphere when it will be discarded.

"The third unit called the LEM will be the ferry that will carry the two astronauts from lunar orbit to the moon's surface and back to rendezvous with the mother craft. It is here that the all-important lessons of rendezvous learned during the Gemini flights pay off. After the explorers climb through the hatch back into the Command Module, the LEM will be discarded and will remain in lunar orbit."

He spoke of future projects and further outlined his thinking as he continued:

"To understand the magnitude of our space exploration, I suppose the best way to impress people is with a physical relationship.

"For example, in the Apollo program we will use a launch vehicle which will have the capability of boosting as much as 120 tons into earth orbit or to speed a payload weighing 45 tons on a trajectory which will carry it to the moon.

"For another example, on Merritt Island, Florida, a few miles from Cape Kennedy, we are constructing a spaceport for launching the Saturn I-B launch vehicle and its Apollo spacecraft on its lunar journey. The entire vehicle is 360 feet tall. It is as high as a 32-story building. It will be assembled and checked out in an upright position, indoors, in a building 520 feet tall. This building has a greater volume than the Empire State Building or the Great Pyramids of Egypt. The air conditioning unit used in this building has the capability to literally reproduce a rainstorm within the building's shell. A tractor crawler, 90 feet square, will carry the vehicle and a 450-foot-tall tower in the upright position to the launch pad, a distance of about four miles.

"Finally, at Houston, Texas, where we of the Manned Spacecraft Center are located, we are building a new Space Center which includes a 33-million-dollar integrated mission control center from which flights from the earth to the moon and other planets will be controlled. While man is making his quarter-of-a-million mile, three-day journey to the moon, the story of his flight will be recorded via telemetry and television in the control center. When he arrives on the moon and for the first time man sets foot on this long-sought objective, his words will be transmitted and recorded in the control center in Houston. And when he makes his return to the earth's surface, which will take about three and one-half days, his return will be directed from our control center in Houston.

"After the moon, greater things are yet in store for us. We can then consider trips to the planet Mars and, if we can learn to accept the high temperatures, maybe to Venus."

Roger explained to the attentive Optimists that in flights such as these, he was talking of man going into space exploration for periods of *years* as opposed to minutes, hours and days. An estimate of the time required for a round trip to Mars is 450 days. He was certain that we will see, in our time, manned orbital stations in space, housing perhaps a dozen men or more over considerable lengths of time. He spoke of the tremendous task that we as a nation have set for ourselves in attempting the conquest of space. The universe is vast, both in the distances involved and in the magnitude of the forces that must be overcome. Roger asserted that there is no technical limitation to man's capability to conquer nature. The only limits are those of the imagination, will power, determination, and the ability to organize for those great tasks. His own imagination, will power and determination were evident as he continued:

"On the earth's surface we have successfully developed and employed a global network capable of tracking our men in orbit. It is capable of communicating with them and other points in the network as necessary, and capable of locating and recovering them after a return to earth. Most important, it has been shown that these capabilities can be accurately and effectively used in real time to aid the astronaut in the analysis of problems and in periods when time-critical functions must be accurately completed.

"A question we might like to explore is, 'Why should we spend our tax dollars on this goal of mankind? Why not let someone else do it? Why space exploration at all?' As tremendous a job as the moon trip is, it is only the steppingstone to space exploration — and why space exploration?

"There are many reasons. One is the increase of our knowledge of the universe. In many ways this reason seems hardest to justify. However, our experience shows that though scientists may investigate the unknown out of curiosity, with no immediate engineering or economic goal in sight, the increased knowledge they derive results in unpredictable economic benefits."

Roger stated that many immediate returns were being found in the new technologies already developed — the utilization of advanced electronic techniques, new materials and novel types of electrical power production. He pointed out that it is difficult, indeed, impossible, to predict the magnitude and scope of all the economic benefits that have resulted from this program.

There were, however, already specific examples. The economic gain from scientific research is coming faster as we progress through the century. In only the sixth year of the space age, in addition to orbiting men and bringing them back safely and inspecting the moon and Venus, there already are specific returns for use here on earth. In the field of weather the ability to predict major activity has been demonstrated. The ability to predict the weather accurately in detail as much as five days in advance could save over five billion dollars annually in agriculture, lumber, transportation, retail marketing and the management of water resources.

He thought perhaps we ultimately will be able to exert control over weather. The economic benefits of that would be unpredictably large. Literally, this sort of thing could change the face of the earth!

He spoke of the Telstar satellites:

"The Telstar satellites are just beginning to reveal the tremendous utility that space has to increase our communication capability. In a hundred years we increased our ability to communicate across the Atlantic by a factor of a thousand. In a few years, in this decade, we can add another thousandfold. This will permit transmission of complete books in seconds and will permit business machines and computers to be tied together in world-wide networks.

"As you all know, in this program we are shooting for the moon, but in so doing, we develop tools and minds and strength for future and greater enterprises. And how much is this worth? If the past is any indication, people tend to underestimate the value of scientific and technological breakthrough.

"The returns have been fantastic, and what remains to be discovered cannot even be envisioned in our wildest dreams!"

Indeed, Roger was a dreamer, but he dreamed of things that were within the grasp of man. And what he dreamed he was willing to do something about. This seems to be what set Roger apart from his peers. He set high goals for himself and then, with the greatest determination, set out to reach those goals.

9

The Making of an Astronaut

The astronauts' training was divided into three parts. The first, termed "academic," was accomplished at Houston and on field trips where Roger completed more than one hundred hours of study in such subjects as geoscience, geology, geochemistry, geophysics, astronomy, etc.

The second part of their training, called "contingency," taught them survival on the water or any portion of land. This training was to provide for the possibility that a craft returning from the moon could find it necessary to make an emergency landing in some remote part of the world. Under such circumstances the astronauts must be prepared to survive off the land until help arrives.

The last phase of training, "operational," dealt with practice in the centrifuge, simulators, helicopters and aircraft which duplicated the sensations and problems which the men could expect to experience in space.

By late June of 1964, Chaffee had completed much of the academic work and had begun survival training. His first trip in this phase was to the jungles of Panama where they were required to live for three days in pairs. They carried no food or equipment except their parachutes and survival kits.

Roger's description of his foraged food was interesting. He described the hearts of palm trees as "delicious," snakes and iguana lizards as "not so delicious," and crabs and land snails as just plain "terrible."

During the survival training Roger's Boy Scout experiences were recalled with appreciation. He always had enjoyed the out-of-doors, and now, once his shelter of palm leaves was made, he felt at home.

The same could not be said of everyone in the group, however, as tersely recorded by one of the *Roundup* reporters from Houston's Manned Spacecraft Center who covered the excursion:

"SUNDAY — Everyone all smiles as two planes depart Ellington. Poker epidemic breaks out immediately. Seven hours later, land in Panama. Only a few smiling faces.

"Much picture-taking. Note temperature in low 90's. Cooler than Houston. Average annual rainfall runs 130 inches. Local USIA man claims 129 inches fell hour before planes landed. Bus across bridge at *eastern* end of canal, Pacific side. Very confusing to see sun rise over Pacific, set over Atlantic.

"MONDAY — Tropic Survival School class starts at 7 a.m. Ten-foot boa constrictor lounging around class room. Various cages of all manner of snakes, reptiles. Nearby fenced area serves as instant jungle. Contains ocelots, tapir, monkeys, birds. Four-foot electric eel puts on 240-volt demonstration. Remind Chuck Mathews to investigate use of eel as backup to fuel cells.

"Instructor emphasizes, 'Man plus equipment plus environment equals survival.' Details jungle hazards. Stresses good neighbor policy with jungle Indians. Demonstrates 12-foot blow gun used by South American neighbors. Some natives can put out candle with poison-tipped dart at 65 feet. Much talk of importance of ethnic contacts. School out at 4:30.

"TUESDAY — Bus to nearby golf course. Chopper into jungle clearing. Instructor points out poison-tipped spiny trees. Chop open palm tree and eat heart of palm. Not bad. Observe inch-long black ants. Poisonous. Chop into water-filled vines. Jungle drinking fountain. Hack through dense undergrowth. Just like movies. Meet Choco Indian family. Invite us to lunch. Always same old menu: Roasted boa constrictor, filet of iguana, tenderloin of wild pig, mangoes, poi.

"WEDNESDAY — Move into jungle for real by chopper. Drop point about five mile southwest of canal. Astros broken up in groups of two. One native or GI instructor to group. Two mile hike to camp area. Surprise snake on way. Matchete-ize him.

"THURSDAY — Up at 6. Make fire. Bug-repellent makes great fire catalyst. Coffee tastes like boiled iodine. Go out and forage for food. Catch seven-inch catfish. Spot C. C. Williams and Rusty Schweickart returning from fishing with couple of three-inch sun fish. Make two lifetime friends by giving them catfish. Slog upstream on tour of all campsites. Conrad spreads word stay may be extended past Friday unless rain comes. Machete-armed astros eye Conrad menacingly. Urge Conrad to keep big mouth shut.

"School director visits camp. Confuses smuggled transistor radio with Indian drums. Note astros looking lean and hungry after dining on iguana stew. School director all smiles.

Rain starts at dusk. Hit hammock second night in row at 7:30 p.m. Wives will never believe it.

"FRIDAY — Astros build big smoky fires in cleared areas for chopper food drop. Also signal chopper with mirrors. Devour C-ration drop with gusto. Canned chip beef, canned fruit, canned crackers. Break camp. Move out. Walk two miles. Inflate Gemini rafts and rendezvous with school boats at prearranged point. Much comparing of beards and chigger bites."

Returning from Panama Roger, with his usual spirit and drive for progress, began the task of beautifying their new home and yard. The lawn was impeccable, and he took great pride in the newly planted, carefully placed flowers and trees. Much-needed relaxation was obtained by this yard work. When he began a new project, it was no half-way measure. In fact, Martha sometimes felt he went to extremes. Knowing and appreciating his creative talent, she asked him to build her a small water fountain behind the house. Roger was happy to oblige, and after hauling tons of gravel and spending days of hard labor, he announced proudly that the task was finished. Martha gazed at the colossus and similingly remarked that they were surely the only family in Houston with a waterfall in their back yard!

Continuing the habit of earlier years, Chaffee made good use of any and all available time. His philosophy was that there was a time to eat, a time to sleep, a time to work or a time to play — and whichever of these he was doing, he did to the exclusion of all the others. He was a good eater, could sleep anywhere, and he worked and played with vigor. He had abundant health, a factor necessary, of course, for astronaut status.

He never lost his love for parties; he enjoyed giving them as well as attending them. They did plenty of both. His love for his family was deep, and he enjoyed his weekends with them, playing with the children in their own back yard with its pool and patio. Often breakfast, lunch or a barbecue was served, depending on the time of day. He also enjoyed inviting the neighbors and their children over to join in the fun, and on occasion he bike-hiked down to the lake for a time of fishing. Circuses and proper shows for the children were often included in their activities. A busy life indeed. Yet, exceedingly satisfying!

The astronauts left Houston in August to begin their desert training near Reno, Nevada. Temperatures there were recorded at 160 degrees on the sand and 91 degrees six feet above the surface. The men removed all their clothing except their shoes and the long underclothing worn under their spacesuits. They then covered themselves with loose-fitting Arab-style burnooses and headed out, in pairs again, for two days in the desert. Again they ate lizards and snakes as they had done in Panama. Only this time wild rabbit was added to their menu — if they were fortunate enough to catch one.

Once again it was rough on the "city boys." One of them was overheard to say, "I would just as soon put on my pants and go home." To the former Scout, it was just another camp-out. He cut a tent from his orange and white parachute and soon was cool and comfortable. A reporter walking by asked him how he was doing. "We're real cozy," Chaffee replied, adding, "Of course it could use some wallpaper!"

During early 1965 Chaffee spent a great deal of time in the study of geology. He visited 13,680 foot Mauna Loa in Hawaii and the Katmai Mountain area of Alaska, studying rock formations and lava flows.

By early June he was back in Houston. Along with Gus Grissom and Eugene Cernan, he was given the job of cap com (capsule communicator) for the Gemini 4 flight in which Lt. Col. Edward White II made his famous walk in space. It was the first time that Grissom, White and Chaffee worked together as a team. It was not to be their last.

The two members of the future Apollo spacecraft team followed progress of the trip, during which fellow-astronaut Edward White stepped from Gemini IV and space-walked for twenty minutes.

The space walk proved the adequacy of the space suit White wore and the gear he carried, including the jet-nozzled space gun, to which was attached a camera. A gold-coated cord fed him oxygen from the spacecraft. He also carried an emergency oxygen pack strapped to his chest. Chaffee and Grissom knew that someday they would be wearing similar gear and performing similar feats, and they watched with envy and wished for their own time "up there."

The trip ended with McDivitt bringing his spacecraft back manually, but the astronauts arrived safely, and a "first in space" had been accomplished — they had bettered the time of the Russian space walk. The event was considered eminently successful, and there was great rejoicing at the space center.

Roger and Gus shared another assignment when the first unmanned Saturn I-B rockets were launched. The two men were sent up in their jets to take motion pictures of a rocket as it rose over Cape Kennedy. They flew at levels between 30,000 and 50,000 feet and came back with excellent pictures of the launch.

Geology training continued, and in July of 1965 Roger was sent to the Askja volcano area of Iceland, a site chosen because it is believed to resemble closely the surface of the moon.

In August he was back in Grand Rapids for another visit to the Lear-Siegler plant and to lecture to the Kiwanis Club.

Roger had his own way of announcing to his parents his arrival in his jet. He used a large church near their home as a landmark, counting off the blocks back to the Chaffee's street. Since their home was gray and impossible to see from his flying height, he looked for the bright pink of the house next door, then made several passes. Sometimes he could even see their car as they pulled out of the driveway and headed toward the airport. By the time they arrived he was usually ready and waiting for them. It was unique, but effective.

During his lecture to the Kiwanis Club, in connection with his thorough geology training, Roger explained, "The moon pilots will bring back rock and dirt samples, but a lot of the information will consist of their observations. For example, you can't bring back a hole in the ground or tell by samples alone whether it was of volcanic or impact origin."

He also predicted, "When pilots have killed the awesome navigation and maneuvering problems of moon exploration, scientists will go along. Right now, though, it is more feasible to train pilots to be scientists."

That visit to Grand Rapids was short, but it was followed by his parents' visit to Houston the following week.

They were delighted with their tour of the town and of the new house. They admired the way Roger had wired the stereo set through all the rooms, installed lights around the swimming pool and built his amazing waterfall. Martha jokingly remarked, "When we light the gas torches around the pool, it looks just like a grand motel."

Roger's growing gun collection impressed them. By the time he had reached this stage in his career, he had a large, wall gun case complete with an enviable collection of guns. He had installed lights in the gun case too.

He took great pride in making his own rifles, ordering some of the barrels and lock works from Belgium and carving the stocks from wood which he had brought back from his trip to Hawaii. He gave two of his creations to close friends but kept a third for his own collection, which also boasted the original 22 rifle received from his parents on his twelfth birthday, a beautiful 300 Weatherby given him by a friend, and an old Army rifle which he had rebuilt for himself.

One gun in the collection had been obtained from Mr. Horn, Roger's father-in-law — a gun so old it was considered worthless. For Roger, it was a challenge. He set to work refinishing and reconditioning it and was able to bring out all the beauty of the original stock and barrel. When he showed it to his father-in-law, the surprised man could scarcely believe it was his ancient gun. Roger had managed to make it a thing of beauty.

Roger loved to hunt and found it very relaxing. He thoroughly enjoyed numerous deer-hunting expeditions in Texas. Part of the fun was in loading his own ammunition, never throwing away a spent cartridge but taking it home for reloading. He had his own scales, scoops, crimping machine, powder and ball.

Occasionally Roger would take the children along to the rifle range for some target shooting. They covered their ears when someone else was firing or put cotton in them when Daddy allowed them to shoot by themselves, memorable experiences for the children.

The astronaut's training continued over the next few months. Then on February 28, 1966, an unfortunate accident claimed the lives of two of Roger's fellow astronauts, Elliott M. See, Jr., and Major Charles A. Bassett II. The men were killed in the crash of their military jet plane. The funerals were held at Arlington National Cemetery with Roger acting as pallbearer for Elliott. This now brought to three the number of United States astronauts who had been killed, Captain Theodore C. Freeman having died in a jet crash on October 31, 1964.

The spring and early summer of 1966 were taken up with operational training, including weightless flight in an Air Force KC-135 jet. By flying a parabolic curve, short periods of weightlessness such as would be experienced in space flight could be simulated. The plane was also able to duplicate 1/6 earth gravity, the same as the gravity on the moon.

Roger also rode the centrifuge which duplicated the gravity forces which would be experienced on the liftoff and the landing.

To practice landing on the moon, Roger attended the Navy Helicopter School at Pensacola, Florida, and also spent practice time in the simulators set up at Houston.

March 21, 1966, brought the preliminary announcement naming the astronauts for the first manned Apollo flight. All of the astronauts were hopeful, as well as apprehensive, as the names of the prime crew were read. Roger, who a year previously had said, "Everybody wants to be first," was especially hopeful.

The announcement finally came: Grissom, White and Chaffee! The three men were elated. "I think we have a good crew, and I think it will be a good flight," was Grissom's first comment.

White said, "We'll all be looking forward to the flight."

Roger remarked, "I'm extremely pleased to be named. I think it will be a lot of fun."

The flight was designated Apollo/Saturn 204 (later Apollo I) and was scheduled to orbit the earth for as long as fourteen days, testing the performance of both crew and spacecraft.

10

Last Preparations

The prime crew for the Apollo I Mission had a wealth of experience behind them. Virgin I. (Gus) Grissom, veteran astronaut named as commander, had piloted the Mercury-Redstone flight, the Liberty Bell 7, and was the command pilot on the GT-3, the first manned Gemini flight. Edward H. White II, pilot of Gemini IV, and the first American astronaut to perform extra-vehicular activity, was assigned the senior pilot position. Roger B. Chaffee, who was to make his first orbital flight, was selected as pilot. Roger was considered to be one of the finest engineers of all the astronauts. The backup crew consisted of James McDivitt, David Scott and Russel Schweickart.

The purpose of the mission was to check out the manned operations and the performance of the spacecraft, ground tracking and control facilities. Eleven experiments were to be conducted, six of which were to be medical, four scientific and one technical. In one experiment the French government was to launch a rocket which would release a sodium vapor trail. This would allow the crew to make photographs which would determine wind patterns at very high altitudes.

The flight was designed as an "open ended" mission which, if successful, could continue as long as two weeks.

On March 24, 1966, Chaffee flew to the North American Aviation Plant in Downey, California, to watch production on the spacecraft. "We're not talking generalities any more," he said happily. "That's *my* spacecraft."

The spacecraft itself was to consist of two parts, the Command and Service Modules which together were given the designation 012. The twelve-foot high, thirteen-foot diameter Command Module would house the three astronauts, and the twenty-two-foot high Service Module was to contain a 22,000 pound thrust engine which would be ignited eight times during the Apollo I flight. The first burn was scheduled to come at 25 hours into the flight, and the last one was to set up re-entry into the earth's atmosphere.

The spacecraft was to be placed in orbit by a two-stage Saturn I-B launch vehicle. The first stage, containing eight liquid propellent engines, would develop 1.6 million pounds of thrust and burn for two and one-half minutes. The second stage was a 200,000-pound thrust engine which would burn for about seven and one-half minutes to insert the spacecraft into a 101 by 153-mile-orbit at more than 17,500 miles per hour.

On the morning of March 25, Roger, back in Houston, was surprised by a summons to appear at NASA Headquarters. Dr. Gilruth, Director of the Manned Spacecraft Center, had called Martha and asked her to be present in his office at the same time, without telling Roger of her invitation. When Roger entered the office and found her seated there, he greeted her with a startled, "Well, hi there! What are you doing here?" Martha responded that she thought they had something to present to him.

At this, Dr. Gilruth stepped forward to pin the Air Medal on Roger and read the following citation:

> The President of the United States takes pleasure in presenting the AIR MEDAL to Lieutenant Roger B. Chaffee, United States Navy, for service as set forth in the following citation: For meritorious achievement in aerial flight during the period 4 April 1960 to 25 October 1962 as a photographic plane commander in Heavy Photographic Squadron SIXTY-TWO. Completing eighty-two classified operational missions of paramount military importance to

the security of the United States, Lieutenant Chaffee contributed materially to the success of his squadron and upheld the highest traditions of the United States Naval Service.

The citation was signed, "For the President, Paul H. Nitze, Secretary of the Navy."

No specific reason was given for decorating Roger with the medal, but it is thought significant that the dates on the citation include his time of duty in the Heavy Photographic Squadron, Jacksonville, Florida, during the height of the Cuban-Russian missile crisis.

In April the two crews went to Chapel Hill, North Carolina, there making detailed studies of the thirty-five stars by which they planned to navigate and which were programmed into their on-board IBM computer.

That summer while watching a launching of a Saturn rocket at Cape Kennedy, Chaffee exclaimed to Martha, "It's going to be a beautiful sight. I can't wait to take a ride on that bird!" The time was soon approaching, with the scheduled launch only a few months away.

On August 26, Roger's 012 spacecraft was sent from Downey to the Manned Spacecraft Operations Building on Merritt Island near Cape Kennedy. There it was placed in a huge vacuum chamber and during the month of September exposed to a thorough series of altitude tests.

Also during August, the Chaffee family from Michigan, including Don, Mike, Donna and family, drove to Florida for the celebration of Roger and Martha's ninth wedding anniversary. As they talked, ate and fished together for several days, they enjoyed immensely the last hours and days they would spend as a complete family. The gathering was gay. The fishing expedition had yielded about twenty trout, and the Holiday Inn motel chef, entering into the spirit of the occasion, offered to cook the fish. This he did, and two beautiful platters of trout graced the dinner table. The chef also had made an anniversary cake. Months later, the family had cause to remember the glad event with particular nostalgia.

In September of 1966 Chaffee, who had just been given an early promotion to the rank of Lieutenant Commander, was named chairman of his former Boy Scout Council's annual membership drive. In speaking to the scouts, Chaffee said:

"Having been named by the Grand Valley Council as honorary chairman of this year's Fall Roundup recruiting effort is a very special honor, for which I would like to express my sincere thanks.

"I am particularly pleased by this selection in view of my past association with the Grand Valley Council Boy Scouts of America, an association which dates back to 1947, when at the age of twelve years, I became a member of Boy Scout Troop 215, in Grand Rapids, Michigan; an association which has contributed greatly to my subsequent success as a Naval officer and as an astronaut.

"You know, it was exciting to me, as a Scout, to know that there were brother Scouts, pledged to the same ideals, around the world, a world which has come a long way since I started Scouting and made my way up through the ranks to Eagle Scout. *You* could even look back at 1947 and say that things were old-fashioned then, but I can't look at Scouting ideals that were taught me then and say that they are old-fashioned. Those ideals put me where I am today.

"Frankly, I doubt if the things Scouting teaches a boy were ever more important than they are today, with today's advances in technology, communications, transportation, and in energy sources. Men's decisions about what to do with these resources become vastly more important. And the decisions must be made by men who hold high values, as duty to God and country, duty to others, and the habit of the Good Turn. The decisions must be made by men of character, who have learned to live and be truly big men.

"Probably the greatest thing a man can say to himself, or have as his philosophy when he has to tackle a tough job, or make a big decision, is the first eight words of the Scout Oath, 'On my honor, I will do my best . . .'

"Yes, on my honor I will do my best. Just eight small words that have an enormous meaning and that can and should become a way of life to every boy and every man.

"The lessons I learned in Scouting have been invaluable to me. And the same lessons and experiences are awaiting each of you. I trust you will avail yourselves of the many opportunities that Scouting offers."

Soon after the Roundup Roger returned to serious preparation for the upcoming Apollo I shot. Unfortunately, there was still some official indecision about the program. There had been ten successful launches of the Saturn IB rocket out of as many attempts, and the first three Apollo/Saturn unmanned launches designated as A/S 201, 202 and 203 had gone off without a hitch. Yet the final decision to man the A/S 204 (Apollo I) launch was not made until the middle of October, 1966, seven months after the preliminary announcement had been made by NASA Headquarters.

In October the prime and backup crews were brought in to participate in the last two ten-hour series of tests, operating the spacecraft as though it were actually flying in the vacuum of space. Roger and his crew completed both the sea level and altitude runs, but the backup crew completed only the sea level runs because of the failure of an oxygen regulator.

Immediately following the altitude chamber tests, the two crews traveled to the Gulf of Mexico to begin egress training. This training was to perfect the means of exit from the spacecraft once it had returned to earth and landed in the water. Each crew was placed in an exact duplicate of the 012 spaceship which was bobbing in the waves of the Gulf. The capsule was then tipped upside down, a position in which the astronauts might well find themselves following a landing. After a few moments in this inverted position, three uprighting bags from the spacecraft recovery compartment were inflated, and within six minutes the craft was upright. Opening the hatches, the crew egressed into life rafts and from there into the waiting slings of hovering U.S. Coast Guard helicopters.

Training continued through most of October. It had been hoped that Apollo I would be launched during the last part of 1966, but on October 27 NASA announced that the mission was to be postponed until the first quarter of 1967. The delay was due to a clogging of water flow through nickel plates in the spacecraft's environmental, control system. It was necessary for the system to be modified, replaced and then retested.

By mid-November other problems were encountered, and a complete rescheduling of the manned Apollo program became necessary. Apollo/Saturn 205, which was to be virtually a repeat of A/S 204, was scratched and made part of a later dual launch with A/S 208. This released the A/S 205 crew of Walter M. Schirra, Donn F. Eisele and Walter Cunningham, who then became the new backup crew for A/S 204.

During the Thanksgiving holiday Roger decided to enter the Nassau Bay Garden Club's annual contest for the most beautifully decorated home at Christmas time. He went at the venture with zest, and the completed display was an original arrangement of lights topped off with Santa and his reindeer on the roof. He had so wired the reindeer with flashing lights that the effect was one of Old Saint Nick being pulled through the air in his sleigh. It was amazingly clever.

Chaffee returned to Cape Kennedy early in December, but there was another delay in the program when a water-glycol (a coolant) leak developed in the spacecraft's environmental control unit. This unit also had to be replaced and revalidated, an exacting task requiring two weeks' time.

On December 15 and 16 the news media was given a detailed briefing on the Apollo program. At that time details of Roger's planned flight were released, and the outlook was promising for an early 1967 launch.

At Christmas time Roger returned home to Houston to learn that he had won the Nassau Bay Garden Club contest for his unusual Christmas decoration, a fitting reward for his originality and hours of hard work.

That Christmas Roger presented Martha with a pin that he and the crew had designed for their Apollo flight. Their original plan had been to take the pins into orbit with them, making a gift of them to the wives after the flight. The men became impatient, however, and decided to give them as Christmas gifts.

Since they had spoiled their own surprise, immediately after Christmas they had gold charms designed that they secretly planned to take into space and then present to their wives. Each unique little charm was an exact duplicate of the Apollo I Command and Service Modules with a little diamond representing the astronaut's position in the craft.

The tradition of taking mementos on the flights dated back to the first space shots. Roger intended to take along both the pin and the charm for Martha and also a box his mother had prepared, containing a family ring usually worn by his father, the miniature Eagle Scout pin, fraternity pin and wings that he had given to his mother. These items were all packaged and waiting to be placed in the cabin at flight time.

During the Christmas and New Year's vacation, invitations were extended to four Purdue graduates who had become astronauts to be guests of honor at the Rose Bowl game in California. The four were Lt. Col. Gus Grissom, Lt. Commander Eugene A. Cernan, Neil A. Armstrong, and Lt. Commander Roger B. Chaffee. It was a great honor. The men, accompanied by their wives, were given a hero's welcome at the Rose Bowl game.

On January 6 the huge Apollo spacecraft 012 Command and Service Modules were delivered to Cape Kennedy's Launch Complex 34. By mid-January, 1967, they were hoisted to the top of the service structure and then electrically and mechanically mated to the Saturn I-B launch vehicle.

A few days later the combined spacecraft systems tests were successfully completed, and the cryogenic hydrogen and oxygen were loaded into the fuel cells. As a final touch, the solid-fuel Launch Escape System was swung into place on top of the Command Module, a crown of security in case of trouble at liftoff. Apollo/Saturn 204 (Apollo I) was ready for its crew!

11

Count-down T Minus 10

At Cape Kennedy, Launch Pad 34, late January of 1967, became the focal point of space interest. Final preparations for the first manned Apollo shot were being carried out in a confident, unhurried manner.

On January 23 NASA released a news bulletin stating that Apollo I would be launched on February 21 sometime between 10:00 a.m. and 3:30 p.m., Eastern Standard Time.

The prime crew of Chaffee, Grissom and White, along with their new backup crew of Schirra, Cunningham and Eisele, had moved to their quarters at the Cape.

The quarters for the astronauts in the Manned Spacecraft Operations Building are not pretentious, but they are very comfortable. Each astronaut in residence has his private bedroom. There are two large living rooms with easy chairs, television and stereo for all to enjoy. They have their own dining room and private kitchen, complete with waiter and chef who tries to prepare anything ordered by the men. There is also a small but complete gymnasium much used by the astronauts in their efforts to strengthen important hand and arm muscles. Adjoining the gymnasium is a sauna bath for the astronauts' relaxation after their workouts. They also have a conference room and laundry facilities. Here the two crews lived during the final weeks of training and dry runs.

News photographers and reporters were more in evidence now, giving the mission an air of optimism that was welcome to all involved in the program. Even the astronauts were more relaxed, and while being photographed in their spacesuits, broke up one session by triggering the mechanism which inflated their bright orange "Mae Wests."

Both crews met with NASA officials on Thursday, January 26, to discuss the simulated launch which was to take place the next day. No major problems were anticipated. Often before, they had run through their prelaunch procedures while strapped into their spacecraft. The notable differences on this run were that the spacecraft was now perched 200 feet in the air atop their Saturn I-B rocket and that they were to be on their own internal power.

It was decided to end Friday's rehearsal with a practice emergency exit from the spacecraft. To the astronauts it was a familiar procedure. Ed White would reach over his shoulder and unlock the six lugs holding the inner door. Gus Grissom would then help him lower the door to the floor. The outer hatch could then be removed, and they would exit in the order of White, Chaffee and Grissom. The whole exit operation was expected to take approximately ninety seconds.

The countdown began at 6:00 a.m., Friday, January 27, 1967. It was to be a casual rehearsal, a time for the crew to get the feel of working with the other personnel, a time for mistakes, reruns and explanations.

The prime crew was up early that morning. After a good breakfast they strolled through the office adjoining their quarters and chatted with the head of the office, Mr. Friedlander, his assistant, Tom Lane, and the two astronaut secretaries, Lola Morrow and Judy Boen.

They then continued down the hall to the pressurized white room. This room, under Tom Lane's supervision, was kept so clean that there could be 100,000 particles in a cubic foot of air no larger than 5 millionths of an inch. There they began the tedious job of suiting up for the trial run. It was decided that only one astronaut would need the sensors which monitored heart and pulse attached to his body, and the lot fell to White that day.

After the application of the sensors the men donned their undersuits and then sat in the large comfortable suit chairs in front of three test stands where they finished suiting up. The spacesuits were then tested and the oxygen hoses attached. At this time the men breathed oxygen at the test stands to eliminate the nitrogen from the blood stream. From that time on they breathed only pure oxygen.

After all the suiting and testing was complete, the men attached their oxygen hoses to their portable oxygen canisters and walked casually down the hall to the main elevator which Tony Broadway, the building superintendent, had reserved for them ten minutes earlier.

Lola Morrow watched Roger walk down the hall that day, remembering the first time she had seen him as a new astronaut three years before. Roger at that time was the second youngest astronaut, only twenty-eight years old. She recalled thinking how boyish and out of place he had looked to her then and how quickly that impression had faded as she discovered his knowledge of the program. She knew him now as a real engineer and well remembered the day some visiting civilian engineers (who thought astronauts were more fly-boys than engineers) had cornered Roger in his office. Lola's comment then was, "Roger nailed them to the wall," and when they quietly left the office, she had thought to herself, "You asked for it, boys; you're dealing with a cool customer." She recalled that Roger was greatly admired for his engineering skill and was known to be very polite and cooperative.

The men entered the elevator, and, as was his habit, Tony personally took them down to the main floor. On their way down Tony talked briefly to them about the duck-hunting trip which he and the astronauts were planning for the following week. He assured them that he had their guns ready and that everything was set to go.

They left the elevator and the building and entered a waiting truck which conveyed them from Merritt Island to Cape Kennedy and Launch Pad 34.

The atmosphere there was relaxed. Even the Pan American

World Airways fire rescue crew had been omitted from duty. There was no sense of danger. Thirteen successful space flights had been completed, and extra precautions for this routine practice simply had not come to mind.

Roger and the crew were slated to enter the spacecraft at 11:00 a.m., in order to simulate a 2:00 p.m., lift-off. Problems in the ground support equipment, however, detained them until 1:00 p.m. They then crawled through the open hatches and settled in their contour couches with Grissom on the left, White in the center and Chaffee on the right, next to the communications equipment. They worked for some time with the hatches open and then at 2:50 p.m., finally were sealed in.

The cabin pressure was increased to 16.2 pounds per square inch of 100 per cent pure oxygen. The dangers and advantages of oxygen were well known. Pure oxygen would not burn, but there was always a danger at high pressure because the oxygen would rapidly feed any existing fire. A short or a spark was a particular danger in a spacecraft with nearly twenty miles of electrical wiring, plus multitudes of switches and connections within its confines.

The advantages of pure oxygen over a nitrogen-oxygen mixture were two-fold. First, it would save about 500 pounds in weight, and second, it would eliminate the need for a decompression compartment to remove the nitrogen from the blood stream before allowing an astronaut to leave his spacecraft in space.

The countdown continued intermittently throughout the afternoon as minor problems were discovered and corrected. One of these problems was in the communications system. The men were beginning to tire, and Gus Grissom, known for his humorous asides, spoke into the intercom, "Hey! How do you expect to get us to the moon if you people can't even hook us up with a ground station? Get with it out there." Shortly after 6:00 p.m., at T minus 15, the spaceship was switched to internal power. Five minutes passed, and at T minus 10 yet another hold was called to check the highly combustible glycol coolant used in the environmental control system and to switch some of the electrical equipment.

Paul Donnelly, Test Director, announced that the hold would last for ten minutes. Everyone relaxed.

Then at exactly 6:31 p.m., EST. Roger's voice came, "Fire! I smell fire!"

Everyone jumped in unbelieving panic. Two seconds passed, and Ed White called sharply, "Fire in the cockpit!"

Three more seconds passed, and another voice, this time unidentified, shouted, "There's a bad fire in the spacecraft!"

Approximately seven additional seconds went by, and then some undefinable shouts and movements were heard. Another four panic-stricken seconds passed then Roger's last frantic cry was heard, "We're on fire! Get us out of here!"

Ed White was the only astronaut with biosensors monitoring his heart and pulse. Twelve hundred miles away in the Manned Spacecraft Center in Houston, Texas, Flight Director Christopher Kraft and his team watched in horror after Roger's first call. The telemetry dial beat for fourteen seconds and then dropped to zero.

"Mission Accomplished
The briefing over —
They enter the vastness of time
Where in everlasting orbit
They lock onto eternity."

12

"Three Valiant Young Men . . ."

Astronaut Donald Slayton had witnessed the disaster from the blockhouse 1,000 yards away. Fifteen minutes later he called Houston and instructed Deputy Director George Low to assign astronauts to deliver the heart-breaking news to the wives of the crew.

NASA deliberately issued a vague press release until the next of kin could be notified, and the first Associated Press bulletin said simply:

> An accidental fire has broken out on the Apollo launch pad, killing at least one person. The space agency says its victim may have been one of the three astronauts scheduled to take the trip.

Charles Conrad was given the task of breaking the news to Mrs. White. Dr. Charles Berry and Mrs. Slayton informed Mrs. Grissom. Astronaut Michael Collins was summoned to tell Mrs. Chaffee.

While the nation waited in deep concern for further news, another vague Associated Press bulletin was released:

> One of the three Apollo I astronauts has been killed in an explosion or fire on the spacecraft's launch pad at Cape Kennedy. There is no immediate indication as to which of the astronauts was the victim.
>
> The three scheduled to make the trip were Virgil Grissom, Edward White and Roger Chaffee. The victim was believed to be a member of the prime Apollo I crew.
>
> Space agency officials say the victim's name is being withheld pending notification of next of kin.

Roger's parents first received word about 8:00 p.m., when Michael Collins called to inform them of the tragedy. A short time later, the official telegram was received. It read:

> I deeply regret to inform you on behalf of the United States Navy that your son LCDR Roger Bruce Chaffee, USN, died on 27 January 1967 at Cape Kennedy, Florida as a result of a flash fire during an Apollo Saturn 204 mission. His wife has been notified and requested to inform the Navy concerning her desires regarding disposition of remains. It is suggested that you contact her as to details concerning funeral arrangements. Your son died while serving his country.
>
> If I can assist you in any way please wire or write to Commandant, Eighth Naval District, New Orleans, Louisiana. I extend to you my sincere sympathy in your great loss.

The wire was signed by Pierre N. Charbonnet, Rear Admiral, USN, Commandant, Eighth Naval District.

Now it was time to release the story to the waiting nation. The next news release read:

> America's three prime Apollo astronauts were killed at Cape Kennedy during a test tonight. The three men were inside the Apollo spaceship atop a Saturn rocket when it was engulfed by flames. The astronauts, wearing spacesuits, were apparently trapped inside the spacecraft.

Now the nation knew, and it mourned. Condolences began arriving from all over the world.

President Johnson made an immediate statement. "Three valiant young men have given their lives in the nation's service. We mourn this great loss and our hearts go out to their families."

Vice President Hubert H. Humphrey, Chairman of the National Aeronautics and Space Council said, "The United States will push ever forward in space, and the memory of these men will be an inspiration to all future spacefarers. The deaths of these three brilliant young men, true pioneers and wonderfully brave, is a profound and personal loss to me. I have had such close relationships with them that my sorrow is very deep. My heart goes out to their families and loved ones."

The comment of Secretary of Defense Robert S. McNamara was: "Our brave men in uniform, whether in Vietnam or seeking the frontiers of the future, mourn with all of us the tragic loss of three gallant and dedicated American airmen. To the families of Lt. Col. Grissom, Lt. Col. White and Lt. Commander Chaffee we send our deepest condolence."

United Nations Secretary General U Thant said, "The spacemen of our times are all courageous pioneers and they unavoidably face great risks which they take in behalf of all mankind. I know that the international community which the United Nations represents mourns these three deaths and appreciates the sacrifices which these men have made."

The statements continued.

James E. Webb, Administrator of the National Aeronautics and Space Administration commented, "I have extended my sympathy and that of all employees of NASA to the families of the astronauts. The nation feels a great sense of loss. That feeling is even greater among those of us who worked with those competitive young men who were so completely devoted to enlarging man's capability in space flight."

Dr. Robert Gilruth, head of the Manned Spacecraft Center in Houston, Texas, had this to say: "All of us at the Manned Spacecraft Center feel this loss very deeply. I met Gus Grissom in April, 1959, and sweated with him through each of his two flights. None of us will ever forget Ed White's walk in space."

Former President Dwight D. Eisenhower remarked, "The accident that took the lives of three of our highly trained, skilled and courageous American astronauts is a tragic loss to our entire nation. Mrs. Eisenhower and I send to their families our deepest sympathy. Our thoughts and prayers are with them."

Paul T. Hellyer, Defense Minister of Canada, stated: "We are shocked and saddened by this tragic loss of the young men who have contributed so much to space exploration and the advancement of man's knowledge of his universe."

Governor George Romney issued a proclamation of mourning for the state of Michigan and said, "In Roger Chaffee's passing, Michigan has lost a native son who stood on the threshold of space."

In Wyoming, Michigan, where the senior Chaffees now reside, Mayor Edward Weist declared a five-day mourning period and ordered all flags flown at half staff.

Mayor Christian Sonneveldt proclaimed a two-day period of mourning with flags at half mast for the city of Grand Rapids.

During the night following the tragedy, sleep escaped the families of the astronauts. It was during this time that Roger's father penned the poem in the prologue of this book. He also wrote the following poem that same night:

> "Your passage through this
>   life of its few years
> Left its mark of tolerant
>   generosity on
> Those who were fortunate enough
>   to enjoy your friendship
> That will live through this
>   generation
> And many generations
>   to come.
> "You were always ready to
>   help, no matter what
>   the need,
> And all the while the
>   recipients
> Enjoyed your kind and
>   tolerant smile.
> Oh! Great immortal soul—
>   march on."

On Saturday Donna joined Mr. and Mrs. Chaffee for a brief press conference at which time it was announced that they would attend memorial services at the Webster Presbyterian Church, Webster, Texas, on the following day. Mrs. Chaffee said merely, "All we know is that Rog is gone. We're just waiting now to hear what has happened. As long as he had to leave us, I know he is happy it was in his spaceship."

Mr. Chaffee added, "We were conditioned for things like this, but it's still an awful shock. We believe he has contributed a great deal to the nation. He was so energetic, so enthusiastic about this program. Roger was doing what he wanted to do. What is learned by this will help the future of the space program. The price of progress comes high at times. God bless you, Rog."

The memorial services were held at 5:00 p.m., on Sunday, January 29, at the Webster Presbyterian Church. Martha, Sheryl and Stephen were there, joined by Roger's parents, Donna and her husband. Many astronauts, officials and other friends attended the service, including former astronaut John Glenn.

"Nearer, My God to Thee" echoed through the sanctuary, and the Rev. Ernest A. Dimaline delivered the following message:

"In the book of Genesis, when God has created all things and has put men upon the earth, the book says, 'God blessed them, and God said unto them, Be fruitful and multiply, and replenish the earth and subdue it; and have dominion over the fish of the sea and over the fowl of the air and over every living thing that moves upon the earth.'

"We have come today to memorialize a man who believed this with his whole life, a man who took as his life's purpose to subdue all challenges and questions. He believed with his whole life that it was his duty to subdue the earth and have dominion over all things, to make all things serve his questing spirit, to put a name to all things. This is man's purpose because man is the highest form of creation now known to us.

"He, whom we memorialize, believed that it must be man's duty to create, discover, search, find answers in order to fulfill 'this high calling.'

"Roger Chaffee was a man called of God to fulfill this high and holy purpose.

"We come to memorialize a man who was one of many who have dreamed dreams, seen visions, and have gone out to fulfill 'this high calling.'

"We speak of a man who gave his life to point a way, to dare men to see farther than they might have the courage to look, to suggest by his efforts that we have just begun to envision the possibilities of our vast destiny.

"A guide once conducting a group of us through a great cathedral said of the cathedral at the end of the tour, 'Truly a monument to the glory of God.'

"Roger Chaffee and those with him are some of the first of those who have begun the work of another kind of cathedral, a building, not of stones, to sit forever unmoving in one spot, but one which will reach into an endless space, to search out, to find, and to create to the glory of a God who has given us this never ending task.

"By Roger's life and death he has given us a lesson, has shown us that a life so dedicated can, in a few short years, be a monument to the glory of God — the beginning of a sort of cornerstone for the building of a wondering, searching, daring cathedral to God's eternal purpose. For only as a man takes this task upon his life — to subdue his problems, to answer his questions, to have dominion over fate and chance — can he truly glorify God.

"Somehow, Roger's youth says to us: We must never grow old beyond the point of flexibility; we must never grow old beyond the point of growth in mind and spirit; that our minds and hearts must stay young enough to dare all things, to envision the impossible, to reach for the eternal.

"His life would say to us that we should never be comforted, but we should be challenged, dared to go beyond the limit of ourselves, to reach eternally into the future.

"His questing spirit would say to us: Go with God, search out His cathedral of the mind and spirit and of the eternity of an infinite space.

"Roger Chaffee had a high calling. He was a man called out by God. We would do well to so dedicate our lives to follow in his footsteps."

Then came the sound of planes, as three astronauts flew over the church in perfect formation — perfect but for that one slot, left empty in honor of their comrade.

On Monday a military honor guard transferred the fallen astronauts to a C-135 jet transport at Cape Kennedy. In a short time the sleek plane landed at Andrews Air Force Base in Washington. Edward White's coffin was taken to a funeral home in Highland Falls, New York, to await burial at 11:00 a.m., Tuesday at West Point. The coffins of Chaffee and Grissom were transferred to Arlington National Cemetery where Lt. Colonel Grissom was buried at 9:00 a.m., Tuesday, January 31, 1967.

At 1:00 p.m., Roger's flag-draped casket was taken from the Arlington Administration Building, where it had remained under honor guard through the night, and was placed by six Navy enlisted men aboard an artillery caisson. It was then drawn into the cemetery by six horses, three of them riderless.

It was a crisp January day, cold, but sunny. In the quietness the Navy Band softly played hymns, "Faith of Our Fathers," "Abide With Me," "Holy, Holy, Holy" and "Onward Christian Soldiers." Hoofbeats sounded clearly through the music, along with the solemn creaking of caisson wheels.

The caisson, flanked by Roger's fellow astronauts, Michael Collins, Walter Cunningham, Donn Eisele, Richard Gordon, Alan Bean and David Scott, as pallbearers, moved along. Just so had Roger once walked beside the body of his friend Elliott M. See, Jr. Following Roger's caisson was a contingent of sailors and then the procession of family and friends. The first three limousines carried Martha and the children, Mr. and Mrs. Chaffee and Donna and her husband, Richard Young. The fourth car carried Roger's uncle, Robert H. Mosher, an aunt, Mrs. Jay Winans, and House Minority Leader, Rep. Gerald R. Ford and Mrs. Ford.

The cortege halted in front of the grave of Lt. Colonel Grissom. President Johnson, waiting at the gravesite, joined the Chaffees as they stood to watch the pallbearers place Roger's casket next to the fresh grave of his friend.

The family was seated in order: Martha, Sheryl, Stephen, Mrs. Chaffee, Mr. Chaffee. Next to Martha stood Astronaut Eugene Cernan, Roger's close friend and next-door neighbor who had made all the funeral arrangements. President Johnson took his seat next to Mr. Chaffee, and Rev. Dimaline commenced the brief rites. Thrice the stillness was broken; once by the twenty-one-gun salute of the honor guard; once by the mournful sound of taps; once by the shriek of three jet fighters in forlorn formation, bidding a last farewell to their brother astronauts.

At the conclusion of the service the Navy Band played "America the Beautiful" while the sailors, in traditional military manner, removed the flag from the casket, folded it carefully, with precision and presented it to Martha.

President Johnson then arose and greeted each member of the family, expressing to each the genuine sorrow and sympathy of himself and the nation.

A few days after the funeral, all the mementos packaged for the flight were returned. Martha received the pin that had been her Christmas gift and also the small Apollo charm with the little diamond which Roger had kept secret from her. The Christmas pin she wears often, and the miniature Apollo with the diamond pinpointing Roger's place in the craft has now become a part of one of her most prized possessions — a gold charm bracelet containing, among other mementos, Roger's wedding ring; his key to the spacecraft; Tau Beta Pi, National Engineering Society, Sigma Gamma Tau and Phi Kappa Sigma pins; Key to the National Society of Engineers; and his Navy lapel wings — treasures now more dearly treasured.

Mr. Chaffee received the family ring, which he now wears in Roger's memory. Mrs. Chaffee received the miniature Eagle Scout pin, fraternity pin and Navy wings. She has now added to these a pure gold medallion which Roger had planned to take into space before giving to her. The medallion is a copy of the crew's Apollo emblem with the embossed names: White-Grissom-Chaffee, and Apollo I.

The receipt of these items seemed to bring him closer. It was as if his thoughtfulness had transcended the barrier of space that now separated them.

13

In Memoriam

The White House
Washington

Dear Mr. and Mrs. Chaffee:

The nation's sadness and the world's compassion are a measure of the loss you have suffered.

Yet they are no less a mark of the greatness of the cause to which your son was committed, and the size of his achievements in advancing it.

To expand our knowledge of the heavens is to seek a richer life on earth for our children, and generations of children to come. To succeed in that great enterprise we must have men of superior talents, supreme courage and surpassing dedication. Such men are rare, but Roger was among them. He will always be among us, warm in our hearts.

He has done more than stretch our hand into space. He has moved us closer to the fulfillment of an ancient dream, and in doing that he has moved all men closer together.

Mrs. Johnson and I mourn for you as we pray that God's blessing will dwell with you. May you find strength and comfort in the pride that America shares with you.

Sincerely,
Lyndon B. Johnson

Following this letter from the President of the United States came a flood of sympathetic letters, cards and telegrams from all over the world. A few representative excerpts showing the profound shock and earnest concern of a mourning public are herein included:

I wish to express my sincere sympathy in the loss of your son. Knowing it is a great loss both to you, his family, and the nation.

I lost my son, Capt. Iven C. Kincheloe, Jr., in July, 1958. He too was a test pilot and was just thirty years old July 2nd that year. It is hard to understand why young men so dedicated have to die but we who are left behind have to accept it and remember they were doing what they believed in and wanted to do. I feel that out of their deaths something good must have also been done. God has His reasons.

Sincerely,

Mrs. Iven C. Kincheloe, Sr.

It is with great sadness I write this note. Words cannot express the sorrow we feel for you all at this time.

We had been following with great pride Roger's career and were so hopeful for his upcoming flight.

I told Jeff and Robin, "Mom used to play with him when I was a little girl. He used to tag his sister and me around as we played."

Sincerely,

Hope Perdue (Nelson)

For some time I have sat here trying to think of some adequate way to express my condolences. I have concluded that there is none.

All I can say is that Mrs. Hart and I are keenly aware of the anguish you are suffering. And, with the nation, we extend our deep sympathy.

Sincerely,

Philip A. Hart

United States Senator

Three years ago I became an Eagle Scout and was a member of the Lt. Roger B. Chaffee Eagle Graduation Class. Even though I never met him, I have felt great pride in the fact that I was in his graduating class and considered him a personal friend.

I would like to attempt to offer some consolation in the

moment of great personal loss. Not only have you lost a son and Mrs. Roger Chaffee a husband, the whole country has lost a great man.

Sincerely,
Roger A. Stam

We are the parents of Don Lind, another of the astronauts, and have wanted to write and express our deep sympathy at the loss of your son Roger Chaffee.

We know some of the other feelings you have had. Pride in the efforts he was making to advance the technology of our country. Pride in his dedication to a program. Pride in his courage to travel into the unknown.

We have not yet known the feelings that come when a mission is assigned, as you have known, but we feel sure this pride must reach its height at such a time.

Your loss, of course, we cannot comprehend. May it be some comfort to you to remember that he was doing the thing he wanted most to do. Few men have the opportunity to leave a worthwhile legacy to the human family as he has done. Above all, that he died as a man, with courage to do his best to the end. "Greater love hath no man than this, that he lay down his life for a friend," (or a cause).

With love,
Leslie and Elizabeth Lind

May we extend our deepest sympathy to you at this time. Our hearts are heavy over the loss of Roger as he was friend and classmate to both of us. We followed Roger's career with such pride and we mourn him too.

My husband was in the class of 1952 and I graduated with Roger in 1953. We are very hopeful that a memorial scholarship will be set up from our class to help some young man to attend college. Roger's life held so much meaning and should be an inspiration to this new, young generation.

Sincerely,
Dr. and Mrs. Thomas Klein
(Shirley Humphrey Klein)

We, the members of William Alden Smith, Jr. Chapter No. 2, Disabled American Veterans share your sorrow for the loss of your beloved son, Roger, a fine and courageous astronaut. The loss of your son is also our loss and the nation's loss as well.

Please accept our heartfelt sympathy, and may God bless his soul.

> Yours very truly,
> Disabled American Veterans No. 2
> Carl N. Simmerer, Commander

. . . I am flying F4 Phantoms near San Diego preparing for carrier deployment. Unfortunately Roger and I never had many opportunities to meet while we were in the Navy and recall our many experiences shared at Camp Shawondossee and in Scouting. It was my good fortune to know Roger during those years and I want to report to you that his outstanding character, dedication, and high ideals have often been inspirational to me. In the past I have found strength in the remembrance of Roger's example and I am sure that I will find even more opportunities in the future.

I extend to you my deepest sympathy and pray that God will graciously comfort you, Martha, and the children.

> Sincerely,
> Jim Curry

My sincere condolences at this sad time in your lives. I didn't know Roger very well; but what contact I did have with him at Central (where he was a year ahead of me) was always most pleasant and friendly. You have every right to be proud of your son.

> Most sincerely,
> James A. Stegenga, PhD
> Professor, Ohio State Univ.

This from Steven Farrell, the son of Roger's department head at Herpolsheimer's Department Store:

I'm sorry about your son's accident. He gave his life so boys like me can have a safer journey into space someday.

I am the proud owner of the letter which he wrote. It hangs above my bed. Maybe this letter will help me as I grow up.

And still they came.

Enclosed you will find letters of sympathy and concern from the children in our first grade. They want you to know that little people of the United States also send you their prayers in your sorrow.

The writing may look a bit strange to you. This is because these children are learning to read and write in a new method called I.T.A.

"deer Mr and Mrs Chffee. ie am sorry ywr sun died. hee wus very braev. the uther men wer braev tw. thae helpt us very much. yw gaev ywr sun tw our cuntry. thank uw. our thauts ar with yw."

Among the numerous telegrams received were two from Washington, D.C.:

Mrs. Griffin and I extend our deepest sympathy in your bereavement. The whole nation mourns the loss of your heroic son and his brave companions.

Robert P. Griffin
U.S. Senator

And,

From the bottom of our hearts we extend to you our deepest sympathy. We were so proud of your son and his outstanding record. If there is anything we can do in this hour of tragedy, please call upon us.

Betty and Jerry Ford
U.S. House of Representatives

All over the land, memorial tributes were paid to the fallen astronauts. Radio station WRLD in Alabama aired the following editorial:

It has been said that a brave man wants no charms to encourage him to duty, and the good man scorns all warnings that would deter him from doing it. Last Friday night we lost three of this country's bravest young men to an accident that seemed too simple and too ordinary for their dedication and bravery. Without fanfare, they were doing their job. They each were aware of dangers inherent in that job, and as best they could be, they were prepared for the time when something would happen that would spoil their record of safety. But most Americans were not prepared for so terrible an accident, and the reality of it will not soon be realized. Most of us had accepted the fact that one of our astronauts would one day be lost to an unforeseen occurrence, but we thought it would be something out of a Buck Rodger's adventure.

Virgil Grissom, Edward White, and Roger Chaffee will never set foot on the moon, but the supreme sacrifice they made will be a steppingstone for others to follow. As taps is sounded over their graves for the last time, the work they loved will be continued. Their knowledge, their experiences are lost forever, but their names will be an eternal reminder of the greatness of their effort.

We cannot express our feelings of compassion over this tragic loss, for we realize our understanding of it is meager. The words that have already been said and written about the tragedy have fallen pitifully short of expressing a nation's sorrow and a nation's respect. In reality, it is not our task to put flowery words together for it is we who are to be pitied. The families, the friends, and the fellow-workers of those now lost to us have accepted the deaths with more bravery than ever we can muster.

The suddenness of the fire that killed the three astronauts caught us unprepared to accept it. With great admiration we can only reflect on their accomplishments. With envy we reflect on their bravery. And with a deep sense of pride we remember that they were Americans. When the race to the moon has been won, we hope Americans will remember three who now belong to the Earth.

Radio and T.V. station WOOD in Grand Rapids, Michigan, ran a four-day editorial. Here are a few excerpts from those broadcasts:

Roger Chaffee, the astronaut, will be buried with full honors at Arlington National Cemetery tomorrow. The nation recognizes the loss of pioneers like Chaffee and Grissom and White. Chaffee was one of the rare breed of men who possessed the intelligence, the daring, and the ability to pioneer in the aviation of space. More than that, he was the kind of man we want our sons to be . . . one of thirty men who returned to us a heartwarming pride in our country. Our children's children will read about Roger Chaffee — and they will call him a pioneer.

A national magazine says:

". . . the conquest of space symbolizes one of man's oldest, most basic drives: the hunger for knowledge, the lure of every new frontier, the challenge of the impossible. That is the legacy left behind by . . . Roger Chaffee."

The lure, the hunger and the challenge, and one of the men who tried to make it a reality should be remembered. One thing that could be done is to rename Kent County Airport in honor of Roger Chaffee. Chaffee did more than go to the moon. He gave his life for that dream. Chaffee gave all that he could give to tomorrow's aviation.

Moving tributes, all.

On January 31, 1967, Central High School in Grand Rapids presented a Memorial Service for Roger. The program, carried by a local television station, was very meaningful to the people of the area. Roger was a product of their schools, their city, a son now mourned.

The student body bowed in a period of silent prayer. The acappella choir sang the words, "Let there be peace on earth and let it begin with me." Then the principal, Mr. Romulus V. Romani, read a theme Roger had written while in the eighth grade at Central (see Chapter 3) and spoke of his personal memories.

> I knew Roger first as a seventh grade student, and later I coached him in football. He was a very clean-cut, polite, sharp boy who worked hard in his classes. He never asked for special privileges and always did his assignments. He was a very good student in most areas but outstanding in the sciences.
>
> He set his sights high, as high as the moon!

In the entranceway of Central High School now stands a "Freedom Shrine" dedicated in Roger's name. It contains twenty-six freedom documents.

The Central yearbook for 1967 was also dedicated to the school's now famous graduate. The dedication reads:

> Yes, the goals were great and the danger ever-present; yet your courage and patriotism led the way. Because your spirit stands as a pillar of human strength and dedication, the yearbook staff consecrates the 1967 *Helios* to you, Lieutenant Commander Roger Bruce Chaffee — a personage among people.

Soon after the assembly Roger's classmates, the alumni of 1953, organized the Roger B. Chaffee Memorial Fund. Their goal was $25,000. This would enable them to award a yearly $1,000 scholarship to deserving young students desiring to prepare for a career in the field of engineering.

On May 19, 1967, the Memorial Fund Committee sponsored a program at the Grand Rapids Museum in which the planetarium was officially named the "Roger B. Chaffee Planetarium." The guest speaker for the ceremony was Astronaut Eugene A. Cernan, Roger's close friend, who also presented a model of the Apollo/Saturn to the museum. Mr. Chaffee also made a presentation to the museum at that time, a pair of Roger's flight boots.

A second scholarship program was established by Purdue University as described in the following letter written to Martha and the children from the president of Purdue.

My dear Mrs. Chaffee, Sheryl, and Stephen:

Millions of Americans admired and will long remember the skill, courage, and dedication of your late husband and father who was one of America's pioneer astronauts, but no other group admired him more or was prouder of him than the students, faculty and alumni of Purdue University.

All of us who belong to Purdue University desire that he and his brother astronaut, Gus Grissom, be honored and remembered as long as Purdue University stands. To this end, the Board of Trustees of Purdue University has established, and will provide when the time is appropriate, full scholarships (tuition, fees, room, board, and books) for Sheryl and Stephen, should they wish to follow in their father's footsteps as students of Purdue University.

Further, the Treasurer of the University has established a special fund designated the "Astronauts' Scholarship Fund" in memory of Lieutenant Commander Roger B. Chaffee, USN, and Lieutenant Colonel Virgil I. Grissom, USAF, gifts to this fund to be used to provide scholarships for Purdue students whose career objectives in engineering, science, and government will contribute, directly or indirectly, to the nation's space program. All scholarships awarded from this fund during the years ahead will be designated as Roger B. Chaffee Scholarships or Virgil I. Grissom Scholarships. While most of the gifts and contributions to this scholarship fund will come directly to the University, some will be made through the Purdue Alumni Scholarship Foundation. All such gifts will be pooled, however, in the administration of these scholarships.

Further, the Board of Trustees will, at its meeting on 1 March, formally take official action to name the administration building at Purdue's Jet Propulsion Center after your husband and father and the building housing Purdue's School of Aeronautics, Astronautics, and Engineering Sciences after Colonel Grissom.

. . . Finally, I know that what others do or say cannot assuage the deep sorrow that is yours to bear, but Commander Chaffee's memory will be cherished and kept bright at Purdue University, which he loved, too.

Yours sincerely,

Frederick L. Hovde
President

"Roger B. Chaffee Hall" is considered one of the foremost jet propulsion laboratories in the country. It is used for graduate training in aerospace engineering by the Purdue students and for research by NASA. The Air Force, Navy, Army Ballistic Missile Agency and National Science Foundation also use the facilities of the $640,000 office library.

Nearly every state of the union sent scrolls of resolutions which were passed to honor the astronauts. Among them was a tribute given on February 1, 1967, when the state of Michigan declared an official five-day period of mourning and ordered all flags to be flown at half mast. A second resolution read as follows:

House Concurrent Resolution No. 14

A concurrent resolution of tribute to Lt. Commander Roger B. Chaffee.

Whereas, The state of Michigan along with the entire nation was shocked at the tragic and untimely death of one of its honored sons, Lt. Commander Roger B. Chaffee, the son of Mr. and Mrs. Don L. Chaffee of Wyoming, Michigan; and

Whereas, Roger B. Chaffee applied himself with zeal and determination to the task of the initial exploring of space by his dedicated application to the project of putting man on the moon; and

Whereas, Roger B. Chaffee's wholehearted application to this project was with full realization of the risk involved, but determined that the benefit to mankind was well worth it; now therefore be it

Resolved by the House of Representatives (the Senate concurring), That the Michigan Legislature does express for itself and all the people of Michigan their profound pride in the contributions to the space effort and the betterment of mankind made by Roger B. Chaffee and does express its deepest sympathies to Mr. and Mrs. Don L. Chaffee on the loss of their son, and does unanimously join Mr. Chaffee in his father's farewell "God Bless You Rog;" and be it further

Resolved, That a copy of this resolution be sent to Mr. and Mrs. Don L. Chaffee, parents of Roger B. Chaffee, and to his sister, Mrs. Richard Young.

The concurrent resolution was adopted by a unanimous standing vote.

The state of Florida, in an exceptionally touching resolution, also paid tribute to the astronauts:

IN MEMORIAM

WHEREAS, on January 27, 1967, the United States of America suffered an irreparable loss in the death of three gallant Apollo astronauts engaged in a simulation of the February 21st launch of the first Apollo flight scheduled for up to fourteen days in orbit, and

WHEREAS, this loss of America's first three Apollo astronauts in the flash fire that trapped the crew in their spacecraft atop a 200-foot rocket during a launch pad test constituted a severe blow to the space efforts and has occasioned the grief and sorrow of our country, and

WHEREAS, this Senate would pay tribute to these courageous men for their gallantry, for the years that they spent in scientific service to their country, and would inscribe upon the records of this Senate a testimonial to the sacrifice that they have thus made and that their families have made for the benefit of all humanity, NOW, THEREFORE,

Be It Resolved by the Senate of the State of Florida:

That the Senate does hereby record this memorial and expression of gratitude and bereavement in the deaths of

Air Force Lt. Col. Virgil I. Grissom
One of 7 original Mercury astronauts

Air Force Lt. Col. Edward White II
First American to walk in space

Navy Lt. Comdr. Roger B. Chaffee
Awaiting his first flight in space.

144

> BE IT FURTHER RESOLVED that the Senate stand
> in silent prayer in memory of the heroism of Lt. Col. Virgil
> I. Grissom, Lt. Col. Edward White II and Lt. Cmdr. Roger
> B. Chaffee, and in sympathy for their bereaved families.

Innumerable other tributes and memorials were made to Roger by the Veterans of Foreign Wars, American Gold Star Mothers, service clubs and other groups. His name was engraved on the Wyoming Park Veterans Memorial Marker, and he was honored at the 54th Anniversary Dinner of the Grand Valley Council Boy Scouts of America.

Permission was requested to dedicate a space park with Roger's name in the state of New York, and an island off the coast of southern California was given his name.

The Grand Rapids Bar Association presented Mr. and Mrs. Chaffee the annual Liberty Bell Award for Roger's "outstanding contribution to our community, state and country."

And the tributes continued.

A memorial in the 1967 yearbook of the Grand Rapids Baptist College reads:

> Risking one's life for mere excitement is foolhardy . . .
> risking one's life for a cause is heroic. Roger Chaffee was
> willing to risk his life for our space program, and on
> January 27 it was asked from him. Once we could name
> him a hero; now we salute him one.
>
> Baptist Bible College could claim no personal ties with
> Roger, but as a part of Grand Rapids we shared in the
> pride of having an astronaut from our town. After the
> Cape Kennedy tragedy we could feel a special, warm pride
> in Roger Chaffee, and in his life — the way he lived it and
> the way he gave it.

The Greenville, Michigan, Library, which Roger and Donna visited as young children, also established a Memorial Fund from which books were purchased and inscribed with Roger's name.

On May 7, 1967, the Nassau Bay Garden Club dedicated a large pine tree as a living memorial to Roger. The ceremony took place directly across the street from the NASA Headquarters building in Houston. Martha and the children attended, along with Dr. Gilruth, Director of the Manned Spacecraft Center and other friends. During the ceremony it was revealed that each year Martha will signal the opening of the Christmas season in Houston by lighting the decorated tree. At the conclusion of the ceremony, Sheryl and Stephen unveiled a granite marker which was inscribed with the words,

In living memory to
ROGER B. CHAFFEE
Lt. Commander-US Navy-Astronaut
Apollo I
May his dedication be our inspiration
Presented 7-May-1967 by the
NASSAU BAY GARDEN CLUB

So often grief inspires poetry, and the impact of this disaster moved many Americans to record their thoughts in this form. The following, written by S. Louise Rayle, is representative of the many poetic tributes paid to the astronauts:

A SALUTE TO OUR ASTRONAUTS

A spark, a call, a frantic plea;
"Quick, get us out of here!"
A fiery flash, a people stunned,
A spaceship brown and sere.

Your rocket stood in readiness —
Just three weeks left 'til "go;"
Within, three dedicated men;
Why did fate treat you so?

You were training for another flight
To explore the realms on high;
With courageous hearts and gifted minds,
And a twinkle in your eye.

So daring, young, and valiant,
With many a lofty plan —
No one could claim you as his own —
You were the sons of Man.

A nation watched each flight progress;
Your hopes, your dreams were ours.
Your joys and triumphs too, we shared —
Your sunshine and your showers.

The anxious moments 'ere each launch,
The thanks for orbit true —
A million eyes glued to the screen!
A million prayers for you!

We listened for your space-sent words
With keen anticipation,
And thrilled with you at views supreme
In joyous exultation.

How oft we've watched as birds winged by
So gracefully and free,
And wished we earth-bound mortals
Might know such ecstasy!

Then forward step our astronauts
To cruise unchartered skies;
Our pioneers of a brave new world
We can but visualize.

Virgil, you made us all so proud —
Our heroic son of space;
And Ed, that marvelous walk up there
Made you our space-age ace.

Roger, you had so many dreams
And loved your work so well;
Our nation had high hopes for you,
Knowing you would excel.

Then, suddenly, your hopes are gone —
Your tethers cut asunder;
Setting soul and spirit free
To roam the wild blue yonder.

Perhaps God in His wisdom,
Will, from His throne on high,
Make you, our space-age heroes,
His guardians of the sky.

Thus, in large and small ways, the memory of Roger B. Chaffee will live on. The feelings of all were aptly described by Roger's pen pal in India, Khursheed Uzzama Khan, who wrote:

A great hero of Michigan whose name will be written in "golden words" in the world's history, and the world, the peoples of United States of America (will) never forget this great hero. I have not words to write about Roger B. Chaffee and his braveness. I will never forget Roger, my elder brother, over Seven Seas in United States, and a great hero of the world who lost his most costly life for his country, the United States.

The most recent and highest award presented to Roger B. Chaffee came posthumously when, on October 23, 1967, Martha accepted for him NASA's coveted award, the Exceptional Service Medal. The only NASA award above this is the Distinguished Service Medal — a medal that may be obtained only by astronauts who have traveled in space. As she accepted the medal, Martha said, "Words seem almost inadequate at this time." The presentation was made by James E. Webb, NASA administrator, at NASA's Washington headquarters. The citation read:

> "The National Aeronautics and Space Administration awards to Roger B. Chaffee (posthumously) the NASA Exceptional Service Medal.
>
> In recognition of his outstanding contributions as an engineer and test pilot to the Apollo manned space flight program. His leadership in improving the conceptual design of and developing operations and procedures for the stabilization and control, environmental control and communications systems of the Apollo spacecraft; the vision and ingenuity he displayed in adapting Apollo ground test equipment for inflight use and his development of operational procedures are recognized as constituting exceptional service of lasting value in the Apollo program."
>
> Signed and sealed at Washington, D.C.
> this twenty-third day of October, Nineteen Hundred and Sixty Seven
>
> James E. Webb
> Administrator — NASA
>
> Robert C. Seamans, Jr.
> Deputy Administrator, NASA

Also present at the ceremony were Chaffee's parents, Don and Mike. For all of the Chaffees — Martha, Sheryl and Stephen; Don, Mike and Donna, the unconquered spirit of their beloved husband, father, son and brother continues to bring inspiration for their own lives.

14

Aftermath

Each of the astronauts shared the desire to have the space program continue should anything happen to him. As has been noted, Gus Grissom had said, "If we die, we want people to accept it. The conquest of space is worth the risk of life."

In answer to a comment about the possibilities of death in the space projects, Ed White had replied, "If it happens, we wouldn't want to hold up the space program. We have to keep progressing."

The wish of the astronauts has been carried out. Immediately following the tragedy a seven-man review board, headed by Dr. Floyd Thompson, NASA Langley Research Center Director, began the task of investigating the accident to determine the probable cause.

The board reviewed the film from the spacecraft's TV monitor and the tapes from all its electrical communications. On February 3 in a memorandum to NASA Administrator James Webb, they revealed that initial investigations by the board showed that no direct indication of the source of the fire had been found. They also announced that the official death certificates of the three astronauts listed the cause of death as asphyxiation from smoke inhalation.

The review board also revealed that they would disassemble Roger's 012 Apollo spacecraft in parallel with Apollo 014 which was flown in from the North American Aviation Plant at Downey, California. It was hoped that by comparing the two crafts as they were disassembled, the cause of the fire might be discovered.

On February 22 the review board issued an interim report which once again revealed that no cause for the blaze could be found. The board had investigated such possibilities as electrostatic, electric short-circuit and even spontaneous combustion of materials in the cabin. The spacecraft batteries and environmental control unit were checked for the chance of chemical reaction. These tests ruled out such a possibility.

Theorizing that the most likely origin of the blaze was an electrical malfunction, the board emphasized that the exact cause may never be known.

In the same report the board offered the following theory as to the route of the fire:

The blaze probably began under Grissom's couch where it burned unnoticed for a few seconds. The astronauts had their faceplates closed and were unable to hear or see the flame. At 6:31.04 EST, Roger smelled the fire and gave the first report to the blockhouse. By 6:31.12, the fire had spread to the nylon netting, velcro patches, and environmental control unit insulation. At 6:31.19, the tremendous heat had raised the cabin pressure to thirty-four pounds per square inch, bursting the pressure hull in the floor under Roger's couch. By this time the water-glycol and oxygen lines had ruptured, spreading the flames even further throughout the cabin.

The board admitted that six years of experience and eighteen-million miles of successful space travel had dulled their alertness to the possibility of a spacecraft fire. Without forethought they had even installed combustible nylon and polyurethane foam material without any breaks to isolate a blaze.

Several recommendations were made by the board in the February 22 report:

—The solid combustible nylon and other flammable materials should be replaced with those that are nonflammable.

—Fire breaks should be placed throughout the cabin.

—All oxygen and flammable liquid systems should be made more fire resistant.

—Full flammability tests on a mockup should be conducted.

—Cabin fire emergency procedures should be revised.

—A new hatch should be designed and installed which would allow for rapid egress from the cabin in an emergency.

There is reason to believe that if an automatic piston type hatch had been in use at the time of the accident, the men might well have escaped. One turn of a ratchet and the door would have been open. The ironic part of the whole matter is that just such an automatic escape hatch was already on the drawing board, and a prototype was in existence at the time of the accident. Had the first manned Apollo shot been postponed for a few months, the new hatch could have been installed and the tragedy possibly averted.

The board concluded its interim report by emphasizing its determination to stay with its philosophy of using pure oxygen instead of an oxygen nitrogen mixture. It also recommended that cabin pressure in flight remain at five pounds per square inch.

The board, however, did urge a re-study of the two-gas system and, significantly, recommended that no more pressurized oxygen tests be conducted during prelaunch exercises.

In April, 1967, the final fourteen-volume report on the Apollo disaster was completed and presented to hearings of both the Senate and the House in Washington. The board revealed many problems in manufacture, quality control, design and engineering. Both the prime contractor, North American Aviation, and NASA officials admitted that the possibility of such a fire was so remote that it was beyond comprehension.

The cause of the fire was not positively identified, but it was thought that a faulty conductor under Gus Grissom's couch arced to another metal object.

The hearings also revealed, to the sorrow of the astronauts' families, that there may have been a great deal of political play in the awarding of some of the Apollo contracts and subcontracts.

NASA Administrator James E. Webb concurred with the findings of the board and stated: "If any man in this room asks for whom the Apollo bell tolls, it tolls for him and me, as well as for Grissom, White, and Chaffee. It tolls for every astronaut test pilot who will lose his life in the space simulated vacuum of a test chamber or the real vacuum of space."

On May 9, 1967, NASA formally announced that the former backup crew of Walter M. Schirra, Jr., Walter Cunningham and Donn F. Eisele would carry on the first manned Apollo mission in the first quarter of 1968.

NASA outlined the following changes that would be made in the spacecraft:

—Stainless steel would replace soldered aluminum lines for oxygen piping.

—Improved methods of assuring good soldering and mechanical joints would be used.

—Wiring runs would be shortened and protected.

—A quick exit, single piece side hatch with pyrotechnic piston actuation would replace the former two piece hatch.

—Teflon, beta cloth, and other non-combustible materials would replace combustible materials in the spacecraft and in the crew's pressure suits.

—Flammable materials which must remain would be distributed so that any fire would remain localized.

—A hoze-nozzle fire extinguishing system would be installed in the spacecraft.

It is inconceivable, in looking back, to realize that there was no fire extinguisher of any type on board the spacecraft!

The decisions to retain the water-glycol coolant fluid in the environmental control system and to continue pressurized spacecraft tests at sixteen pounds per square inch in pure oxygen were reiterated. However, NASA hastened to add that the tests would be run with greater procedural safeguards.

The hearings were over. The lessons were learned. The price was paid. Roger and his comrades had died in the service of their country just as surely as though they had fallen in combat or in space, but they did not die in vain. Their sacrifice was a priceless contribution to their common goal, the conquest of space.

Man will proceed on his "course to the stars." Don Chaffee trusts it will be with the following thought in mind:

"The exploration of the world and the universe belongs to the living; true. But let us not forget the dead, who with their pioneering efforts paved the way."

Stairway to the Stars

Glossary of Terms Used in the Book

Aeronautics. The science that deals with the design, construction, operation and performance of aircraft.

Astronaut. A traveler in interplanetary space.

Astronautical. Belonging to astronautics.

Biosensors. Devices fastened to the body of the astronaut, which report heartbeats, brain waves and breathing.

Biplane. An airplane with two main supporting surfaces, one above the other.

Capsule. A craft which houses astronauts or instruments.

Centrifuge. A machine into which an astronaut is strapped and whirled, causing the body to feel heavy.

Countdown. A time of check-up before launch, when every part and operation of rocket and spaceship is tested.

Crew, back-up. Substitute crew for prime crew, in case of emergency.

Crew, prime. Crew scheduled for space trip.

Flattop. An aircraft carrier.

Gantry. A rolling service station for rockets and spaceships.

Geochemistry. A science dealing with chemical composition of and possible chemical changes of the earth.

Geophysics. The study of the earth dealing with the complex physio-chemical forces acting upon it internally and from outer space.

Geoscience. Any science dealing with the earth.

LEM. Lunar Excursion Module, attached to the spaceship. A ferry to carry astronauts from orbiting spacecraft to moon and back.

Mission. A particular trip into space, such as an Apollo mission.

Module, Command. A unit within the spacecraft to house astronauts during transit from earth to space and back.

Module, Service. The unit within the spacecraft which houses the service mechanism.

N.A.S.A. National Aeronautics and Space Administration.

Parabolic curve. A long, sloping curve similar to an orbit.

Satellite. "Follower," an object which follows another object in an orbit.

Simulator. A machine designed to "simulate," or approximate, conditions of space.

Trajectory. The curve that a body describes in space.

Telemetry. An instrument for measuring the distance of an object from an observer.